The Saints' Guide to

KNOWING THE REAL JESUS

Apostolate for Family Consecration®
Catholic Familyland®
3375 County Rd. 36
Bloomingdale, OH 43910-7903
(740)-765-5500
www.familyland.org

The Saints' Guide to
KNOWING THE REAL JESUS

David Mills

CHARIS

SERVANT PUBLICATIONS
ANN ARBOR, MICHIGAN

Charis Books is an imprint of Servant Publications especially designed to
serve Roman Catholics.

Published by Servant Publications
P.O. Box 8617
Ann Arbor, Michigan 48107

Cover design by Paul Higdon-Minneapolis, MN

01 02 03 10 9 8 7 6 5 4 3 2 1

Printed in the United States of America
ISBN 1-56955-272-X

Library of Congress Cataloging-in-Publication Data

Mills, David, 1957-
   The saints' guide to knowing the real Jesus / David Mills.
      p. cm.
   Includes bibliographical references.
   ISBN 1-56955-272-X (alk. paper)
   1. Jesus Christ—Person and offices. 2. Theology, Doctrinal—Popular
works. 3. Jesus Christ—Person and offices—History of doctrines—Early
Church, ca. 30-600. 4. Catholic Church—Doctrines. I. Title.
   BT203 .M55 2001
   273' .1—dc21

                                                      2001002972

To Hope

CONTENTS

PREFACE

I have always thought prefaces thanking nearly everyone the author knows slightly embarrassing, like the Hollywood star introducing 4,378 of his closest personal friends. Now I understand why writers put them in. Even someone with the vanity and ego of the typical writer or academic learns that without the help of many others, he would not have anything to say. (This doesn't always stop him from writing anyway.)

My reading made ever more clear to me the debt I (and the rest of you) owe to the early Christians, who preserved for us the Gospel, often at the cost of their lives. We would not have it or know it so clearly, had not St. Ignatius and St. Polycarp died for the faith, and St. Irenaeus slogged through all the Gnostic systems to refute them, and St. Athanasius argued with the Arians for decades, even when they kept sending him into exile—not to mention the sacrifices of St. Justin Martyr, and St. Hilary of Poitiers, and St. Vincent of Lerins and ... you get the idea. They are a cloud of witnesses to whom great honor is due.

I must thank my fellow editors of *Touchstone*—Steven Hutchens, Patrick Henry Reardon, Leon Podles, and William Tighe—my friends Fathers Addison Hart, Quintin Marrow, and James Hart, and my colleagues Rodney Whitacre and Leslie Fairfield, who read much of the manuscript and corrected all sorts of errors. (To be fair to them I must admit that I didn't always take their advice.) I should also thank Gavin McGrath, the academic dean at Trinity Episcopal School for Ministry, where I serve, for giving me the time to finish the book. And my editor, Bert Ghezzi.

Finally, I must thank my family—my wife, Hope, and my children, Sarah, Christopher, Hannah, and Jonathan—who endure the weeks when I am, as my wife puts it, "there, but not in any useful sense." It is to her I dedicate the book, for without her I wouldn't have known so well the joys and blessings of an incarnate life.

ONE

THE SAINTS' WORDS

The Christians stood in the sand of the arena, stripped naked, surrounded by thousands of people who wanted them dead. A few hours earlier, the Roman governor had asked them to pledge an oath to the emperor as if he were a god, and they had refused.

The oath was what we would call a legal fiction. It was just a way of pledging to be a good citizen, and no one would think they actually meant it. To give the oath was somewhat like standing at the Olympics for someone else's national anthem. You stand to be polite and to give a general assent to the Olympic ideal. No one would think you wanted to emigrate to France because you stood for the playing of the Marseillaisé.

Yet the early Christians would not give even a fictional assent to a god other than their own. They would have no other gods before them, even a god that was really only a symbol for good citizenship. They were good citizens, but they would not take the oath. And so they now stand in a circle, back to back, with no place to hide, and no way to escape, as large, wild, starving lions circled, and circled, and circled, and finally charged.

One throws out a hand, and the lion snaps down on his arm just above the wrist, cutting through skin and muscle and tendon, and crushing the two bones in his arm. Another turns away as the lion's teeth bite into his shoulder and its claws tear down through the backs of his legs.

That was once the price you paid for knowing the real Jesus. It was the price the Lord had paid for being the real Jesus, so no one was surprised. He had said that the world that hated him would hate his followers just as much (Jn 15:18-20).

That the early Christians might die for knowing the real Jesus explains why they cared so much to say exactly the right things about him: If you are going to die for a man, you want to know exactly who he is.

A Foreign Life

The Saints' Guide to Knowing the Real Jesus will explore the early Christian saints' passion for saying exactly the right things about Jesus. They cared about distinctions and fine points of wording to which few today outside a seminary give two seconds' thought.

Christians who all believed that Jesus of Nazareth is the Son of God fought like stray cats over whether—you may not believe this—the Son is "of the same essence" as God the Father or "of like essence." (The Greek word for "essence," *ousia*, is also translated "being" and "substance.") When you have said that a man born to an average family in a small town in a first-century backwater is God himself, arguing over such fine points seems very, very silly. Yet the earliest Christians would not even *speak* to people they thought had gotten this point wrong.

The question is whether they were right to care so much about words. Today we don't think about words very often and we don't fight over them. To us the early Christians' attitude seems—let us be honest—really, deeply, seriously ... weird. It's not practical. It majors in the minors. It quenches the Spirit. It's unkind. It's divisive.

Did you, for example, stop with surprise three paragraphs ago when you found that a book on knowing Jesus was about how we should think of Jesus? Did the word "knowing" in the title strike you as a bit of false advertising? When we think about knowing Jesus, we tend to think about prayer and devotional exercises and spirituality in general, not theology.

I hope to show you, however, that on this matter—how the words we use to speak about Jesus affect how well we know him—the early Christians were right and we are wrong. I hope to show you that by caring so much about getting the words exactly right, they were helping us know the real Jesus much better. And I hope to show you that unless we do as they did, unless we try to get the words exactly right in a way that just doesn't seem natural for us, we will not know Jesus very well.

Writing After Persecution

Let me give one example of how we differ from the early Christians. Among the bad ideas they had to answer was a Christianized form of the religion we now call Gnosticism. It looked enough like real Christianity to fool many people. (I will explain this more in the next chapter.)

We know much of what we know about Gnosticism from St. Irenaeus' book *Against Heresies,* also called *Five Books on the Unmasking and Refutation of the Falsely Named Knowledge.* He wrote the book about the year 180, when he was the new bishop of Lyons in what is now France. He needed to collect, read, understand, and put in order a wide and confusing range of Gnostic writings before he even began to write about them. The book includes over 220,000 words in the English translation I have on CD. Writing it was an heroic work of scholarship.

Irenaeus did all this work as the shepherd of people who had just been brutally persecuted for their faith and might be persecuted again at any moment. Just three or four years before he started writing, his predecessor as bishop had been beaten to death for the faith. Irenaeus might himself have been martyred as well had the bishop not sent him to deliver a letter to the bishop of Rome.

We know how brutal was the persecution because we have a report from the survivors. The people and then the rulers of the city attacked the Christians with unbelievable ferocity.

First, the mob drove them from the public places, such as the baths and the markets, whose gods they denied. In those days Christians were often accused of being atheists because they did not believe in the gods everyone else believed in. Atheists were dangerous because their unbelief might anger the gods, and then *everyone* would suffer the gods' wrath. Life was precarious, and a god's hissy fit might bankrupt or even kill a lot of people.

Next the mob began to lynch Christians in the street, beating and stoning and robbing them, and then started throwing them in prison. The rulers had the Christians tortured day after day, hoping they would give up their faith.

Sanctus' Death

One of the stories the survivors left was of the martyrdom of a deacon named Sanctus. The rulers tortured him for days, but he would say nothing more than "I am a Christian."

The rulers, "having nothing more that they could do to him,... finally fastened red-hot brazen plates to the most tender parts of his body." Sanctus' body "was a witness of his sufferings, being one complete wound and bruise, drawn out of shape, and altogether unlike a human form ... with his body swollen and inflamed to such a degree that he could not bear the touch of a hand."

Unable to break him, the rulers sent him to the amphitheater, where he had to run between two lines of guards who clubbed him as he went by, suffer attack by animals, and sit in a red-hot iron chair before he was finally killed. Through all this, the crowd "did not hear a word from Sanctus except the confession which he had uttered from the beginning."

And yet, after all this horror, Irenaeus ... wrote a book. He thought he ought to spend a great deal of time writing a book exposing people who said the wrong words about Jesus. He had lived through one of the most brutal persecutions Christians had suffered (worse were to come), knew that the people and rulers might turn on them again without any warning, and still worked very hard to get the words exactly right.

Writing a massive book while the graves of one's people are still fresh is not the sort of thing we are likely to do. We would be calling the moving company. The early Christians did it, though. What Sanctus and the other martyrs confessed with their bodies, Irenaeus confessed with his pen. This is the kind of life and mind we are going to look at in this book.

The Early Saints

The "saints" in this *Saints' Guide* will be those of the second through the fourth centuries, the ones who came first after the apostles and are usually called the Church Fathers. We call them fathers because they established the spiritual home in which we now live, and because we still look to them for guidance and instruction.

Before we begin to study them, we have to decide what we think of the first Christians who lived after the apostles died and whether and how faithfully we should follow them. Christians have traditionally seen them as the people who received the story of Jesus from the apostles and put it in the forms in which it could be safely passed from generation to generation. They developed the mind that knows the real Jesus, the mind that knows how Christians who didn't know him in the flesh can best speak of him.

Yet many modern Christians think that something went wrong between the apostles and the early Christians, that someone dropped the torch. I have just read, for example, an evangelical theologian—a godly man, with whom I've talked at length—who declared that the Christian writers of the second century "thought, no doubt, that they were teaching New Testament Christianity: in fact they lived in another realm altogether."

Another realm altogether—well, that is one view, and you can make an argument for it. But not, I think, a good argument. At least not an argument that overcomes the reasonable presumption that those people who lived so close to the beginning, who were the leaders of a living body guided by the Holy Spirit, who inherited their authority and their teaching from the apostles and the apostles' first followers, who completely sub-mitted their lives to the Lord, whose writings are so obviously wise and so filled with Scripture, got it right rather than wrong.

Remember who it is we are listening to when we listen to the early Christians. One of the first of the saints to whom we turn for instruction is St. Ignatius, the bishop of Antioch who was martyred in Rome about 107. He wrote soon after the last of the New Testament books was written. Tradition has it that he and St. Polycarp were both students of St. John the apostle, that he was either the first bishop of Antioch after St. Peter or the second, and that he either knew Peter well or was taught by people who had known him well.

Another of the saints we have taken as our guides is St. Polycarp, the bishop of Smyrna who went to his martyrdom about 155. St. Irenaeus reported that Polycarp had been taught by apostles and talked with many who had seen Christ. As a bishop, he had "always taught the things which he had learned from the apostles, and which the Church has handed down, and which alone are true."

This is not a matter that divides Protestants and Catholics, this love of the earliest Christians. Most Christians who lived after the Fathers have trusted them. They have been so trusted that their writings have often been the trump card or tiebreaker both sides have tried to use in any argument between Christian traditions.

Take the Anglican tradition, which is the Protestant tradition I know best. Even after the English Reformers split from the Catholic Church, they were always quoting the earliest Christians to prove that they had understood Scripture correctly and Rome had not.

They insisted, in fact, that they and not the Catholics were the true children of the first Christians. The reformed Church of England ruled in 1571 that no one could preach any idea not found in Scripture *and* the Fathers. The English Reformers would not have said the early Christians lived in "another realm altogether" from the New Testament.

The Scholars and the Saints

The early Christians made mistakes, of course, and knowing what they taught is not always as simple as you might think. Read, for example, modern Catholic and Orthodox writers on the role of the bishop of Rome in the early Church, and you will see how difficult the task can be.

The early Christians themselves were not always clear which words were those all Christians must say and which were only different ways of saying the same thing. (This happened at the end of the fourth century, when those we now call saints fought over what words to use of Jesus and the Trinity.) But when the early Christians spoke clearly and spoke together, in them we know we hear the voice of the Lord.

You should know that not everyone would agree with this. This is not a scholarly work, though I hope to say nothing the scholars would dispute. However, skeptical scholars sometimes present as scholarly conclusions claims that actually follow from their skeptical presumptions. They find what they expected to find.

Not all of them look to the early Christian saints as wise fathers to be followed because they followed Jesus and know the way. Some have certain prejudices that have blinded them to what might actually have happened, and what most Christians have believed did happen.

One school of thought, for example, tends to believe that arguments over words were really political maneuvers, by which one party tried to capture the Church for itself. They assume that the Church was at its beginning diverse to the point of being self-contradictory, and that the Bible is a somewhat random collection of texts and therefore a book that readers can assemble, disassemble, and reassemble as they think best.

Therefore, when they examine the arguments of the early days of the Church, they assume that each group was simply arranging the evidence as best served its cause. The faith now called "orthodox Christianity" is, they say, simply the view whose partisans won the political battles.

Other scholars see the development of Christian teaching as part of what was once called "early Catholicism." Almost no one uses the term anymore, but the idea lingers on, because people still want to believe in Jesus—the name still has great "cash value" in our society—but not in the Jesus the apostles and their first descendants presented to us.

These scholars believe that the early Christians made up a Scripture, Church order, and settled belief that Jesus never intended. From the freedom and direct relation to God that Jesus proclaimed, the ancient believers fell into making everyone submit to the authorities and do and believe what they were told.

Sometimes these scholars blame the New Testament writers, who (they say) could not break free from their Jewish assumptions, though St. Paul did better than the rest, and St. James did worse. Sometimes they blame the next few generations, who either feared or failed to understand true spiritual freedom and went back to doing things the legalistic way everyone else did.

In either case, what we know as Catholic Christianity is a big mistake. The Church as we know it is not only a stepmother, but a wicked stepmother.

The Real Problem

The second idea is the real modern problem with knowing the real Jesus, I think. These scholars are only saying in their own way what lots of normal people say in theirs: Binding forms, especially very old binding forms, are bad. We ought to be free, not tied down in dogmas and disciplines and rituals. This is really what Jesus wanted. Remember what he said to the Pharisees about the Sabbath (Mk 2:27).

Jesus, these scholars insist, wanted people to respond to God freely and spontaneously. But very quickly the people in charge, who had the power to get their own way, told everyone that Jesus really wanted them to follow a long list of rules.

The traditional Christian sees these things another way. Being bound to believe a Scripture and follow bishops and hold to a creed aren't impositions upon our freedom, but the reasons we can do anything freely. As one wise man wrote, they only "pin down" the faith in the sense that the skeleton pins down the flesh.

These structures are much more like the wiring that directs electricity from the power plant miles away to your heater and stereo and oven and lights. Jesus gave them to us because he created us and knew that we needed them. Such forms are the channels through which the Spirit he sent us does much of his work.

Jesus was himself the earliest Catholic of early Catholicism. He called disciples, gave them authority to teach in his name (Mt 28:18-20), and even told St. Peter that he would be the rock on whom the church would be built (Mt 16:18). The apostles passed on their offices to others, surely doing what their Lord wanted them to do. Jesus taught a lot of very definite doctrines that he obviously expected his followers to hold and pass on after his ascension, and they did so.

G.K. Chesterton described this contrast in the last chapter of his book *Heretics*. The problem with the modern idea, he wrote,

> is that it is always something concerned with the breaking of bonds, the effacing of boundaries, the casting away of dogmas. But if there be such a thing as mental growth, it must mean the growth into more and more definite convictions, into more and more dogmas. The human brain is a machine for coming to conclusions; if it cannot come to conclusions it is rusty.

The modern skeptic who refuses to bind himself to a system of ideas, who thinks he has outgrown such things, "is by that very process sinking slowly backwards into the vagueness of the vagrant animals and the unconsciousness of the grass. Trees have no dogmas. Turnips are singularly broad-minded."

Against the theory, the quite unproven theory, that at some time very early in the Church's history something went very badly wrong, I will assume that on the matter of getting the words exactly right, something went very right. We've been given a living faith, and it has grown as it was supposed to—it has branched out, you might say.

Were St. Paul himself standing at the back of the hall at the Council of Nicaea 260 years after he died a martyr's death, listening to his successors putting the faith into words they expected everyone to accept, he would have been cheering them on. That apostle of Christian freedom would have approved of their tying down the faith.

You may not have realized that there were so many problems in appealing to the saints. Jesus did warn the first saints that since most people weren't listening to him, they weren't going to listen to them, either. Things haven't changed.

The Saints' Guide

As I said, the saints who will guide us will be those of the second to the fourth centuries. The "knowing" in *Knowing the Real Jesus* will mean seeing him by knowing the right words to say about him and rejecting the wrong words. "The real Jesus" will be the One who is revealed to us in the Scriptures as understood through the tradition of the Church, particularly the great saints of the first four centuries and the ecumenical councils.

The book is written for those who have never met the early Christians or have met them only in passing. I will try to give some idea of how they thought and wrote, and why they cared about the things they did. I write for Christians of all traditions for whom the early Christians are the Fathers whose blessing we all ask.

I am also writing for those who feel that the early Christians' insistence on getting the words right was impractical, quenched the Spirit, and needlessly divided Christians. I am assuming—

because I once felt this way myself and have since met hundreds of sincere believers who have also felt this way—that their vigorous and even "rigid" care for the right words will bother you, may even have on you the fingernails-down-the-blackboard effect.

I am painting in broad strokes and bright colors, in the hope that those who cannot see the early Christians very well will see at least the outlines of the picture. I am leaving out many of the details and fine points, but these would only fill in the picture, not change it.

The book is also written with a sense of gratitude mixed with inadequacy. The early Christians' writings are deep and powerful and wise. Writing about them is like walking into a storeroom of jewels and being able to stick a hand into any bin and pull out the wealth of a lifetime. Whatever setting you give the jewels you've taken will not be good enough for them.

But the storeroom is still open. I hope you will read the book, but I hope also that when you put it down you will go to the early Christians themselves. In this book, we will try to learn how to know the real Jesus as much as possible from their own words, and I hope that you will begin to enter their minds and see the world their way.

Submission to the Saints

This is a work of submission to the saints. I am writing a "Saints' Guide" because the saints are the best people to show us the real Jesus. They wanted to get the words they said about the Lord exactly right, and we should too, whether or not we see the need as clearly as they did.

We listen to the saints so closely because they are a good deal holier than we are, and therefore certain to see much farther and much more clearly than we do. They know the real Jesus and can tell us things about him we don't yet know. The saints are tour guides who have lived in the place they will take us, have even "gone native," when most of us know it only from books or short trips to a hotel on the coast.

We call them "Saint" in print and speech, just as we would stand up if they entered the room. They are men and women to be reverenced. An English bishop once remarked that he could understand why an ardent Protestant he knew didn't want to call the apostle "St. Paul," but he thought the man could at least call him "Mr. Paul."

I don't let my children call adults by their first names. You and I are small children compared with the adults we'll be listening to in this book—with St. Paul and St. Ignatius and St. Polycarp and all the other early saints. We are small children sitting at the feet of the masters as they tell us about their Master. This I find very comforting.

In *Letters to Malcolm*, C. S. Lewis described his grandfather as saying he "looked forward to having some very interesting conversations with St. Paul when he got to heaven," as if they would be "two clerical gentleman talking at ease in a club!" His grandfather didn't realize that meeting St. Paul

might be rather an overwhelming experience even for an Evangelical clergyman of good family. But when Dante saw the great apostles in heaven they affected him like *mountains....* [The saints] keep on reminding us that we are very small people compared with them. How much smaller before their Master?

I've tried to express something of this reverence and famil-
iarity in the way I write of the saints. The saints will be called
"Saint" the first time they appear in a section. The title is a signal to stand up. But after that, they will be called by their names
alone.

We listen so closely to the saints because they know the real
Jesus, and know him better than we do. This ought to set us farther away from them, but instead God has brought them much
closer. Because they know the real Jesus, who has taught them
to love others as he loved them, the saints are not just our
fathers and mothers in the faith, but our brothers and sisters,
and our friends, whom we are privileged to call by name.

TWO

WORDS TO DIE FOR

The early Christians tried hard to use the right words to describe Jesus, even when saying them might have gotten them killed. We think of doctrine as a hobby for the sort of people who like that sort of thing. Theologians like theology the way chemists like chemistry and bird-watchers like birds, or podiatrists like feet.

As hobbies go, it is safer than hang gliding and cheaper than collecting Impressionist paintings. It may do some good, and it probably doesn't do any harm, except to make the man who likes it a bit of a bore. ("Good morning, Mrs. Jones. Lovely weather we're having. I was just thinking about those darn Apollinarians ...")

But it is not, we think, really very useful. Wanting to get the words exactly right doesn't have much to do with the Christian life, once you've gotten the basic idea. Close is good enough in horseshoes, hand grenades, and Christian teaching.

We tend to agree with the elegant, worldly dean of an Oxford college in one of G. K. Chesterton's stories. He inclines, he tells the great detective Fr. Brown, "to the old sentimental heresy, 'For forms of faith let graceless zealots fight; he can't be wrong whose life is in the right.'"

The Modern Mind

Try an experiment. In the early fourth century (about 319), a priest in Alexandria named Arius preached a view of Jesus that many others, including the archbishop, thought was wrong. The difference between them turned on what seems to us a very technical question of the Son's relation to the Father, described in the philosophical language of "generation."

Arius believed Jesus to be the Savior and the Son of God, but worried that by making the Son co-eternal with the Father his opponents were teaching that God could be divided and changed (from one into two), which would mean that he was not the eternal and changeless God we need. The Arian slogan was "There was a time when he [the Son] was not."

Arius solved the problem by declaring that only the Father was completely God, and that he created the Son, for which he made what seems to be quite a plausible biblical argument. Jesus did, remember, sometimes speak as if he were not God, as when he asked the scribes, "Why do you call me good? There is no one good but God" (Mk 10:18). St. Peter had said that God "made Jesus both Lord and Christ" (Acts 2:36) and St. Paul had called Jesus "the first born of all creation" (Col 1:15). The author of Hebrews said that Jesus "became so much better than the angels" and was faithful to God "who appointed him" (Heb 1:4; 3:2).

His theory was also arguably the faith of the Church. To say that the Son was "begotten of the Father," as the early Christians did, did not say *when* he was begotten. St. Ignatius had spoken of Jesus as "the Son of God, 'the first-born of every creature,' God the Word, the only-begotten Son," and Arius' argument seemed to fit this teaching quite well.

Nevertheless, Archbishop Alexander and his brilliant young deacon Athanasius declared that the Son was distinct from yet equal to the Father. As Athanasius said, "If as an offspring the Son be other [than the Father], still he is the same as God." They are one "as the light of the sun and of the radiance is one, and as the sun's illumination is effected through the radiance." Only if Jesus were fully God as well as fully man could he bear our sins for us and bring us into the life of the Godhead. If Arius were right, we would not be saved.

Arius was apparently a talented propagandist who put his ideas into songs that people were heard singing in bars and on street corners. A charismatic leader, he was revered for his ascetic life and must have seemed, from the outside, to be a spiritual hero. Though Alexander excommunicated him when he refused to repent, Arius had influential supporters even among the bishops.

Arius and his theory were condemned in a lopsided vote of the world's bishops at the Council of Nicaea in 325. (This council is now known as the first of the ecumenical or general councils, which represent the entire Church.) The bishops created an explicitly anti-Arian creed, including a word taken from Greek philosophy meaning "of the same essence" (or "of one being," as it appears in the creed we say on Sundays).

Many of the bishops did not want to use a word not found in Scripture, but they accepted it because it was the only way they could rule out Arianism with any certainty. The creed itself said that anyone holding the Arian ideas was to be "anathema," meaning thrown out of the Church. Some translations of the New Testament (Paul used the word in Galatians 1:8-9 and

1 Corinthians 16:22, for example) use "accursed" for the Greek word "anathema," because to be anathema was to be, by your own choice, put outside the body of Christ and deprived of the sacraments, and therefore likely to go to hell if you did not repent.

They Fight On

Despite that defeat, the Arian party continued to fight long after Arius himself died about 336, as Arianism developed (or mutated) into new forms to meet each new challenge. The party gained so many converts that they finally held the majority of the world's bishops.

In 359 the bishops at local councils in the East and the West approved an Arian creed. (These did not become ecumenical councils, because those in authority saw that they were wrong.) It was of this year that St. Jerome made his famous comment that "the whole world groaned and wondered to find itself Arian."

Yet many of those we now know as saints would not stop fighting Arius and his heirs, whatever the bishops said. St. Athanasius, now the Archbishop of Alexandria, risked his life and lost his place several times because he wouldn't stop attacking Arius and Arianism. Other bishops and priests also suffered for their beliefs, and many of the laity left their churches to worship in the deserts because they wouldn't accept Arian clergy.

After a hundred years or so, Arianism finally lost. At the Council of Constantinople in 381, now called the second ecumenical council, the bishops reaffirmed the Creed of Nicaea and added some words to it to rule out more bad ideas. They rejected the local councils of 359. But the Arians—now called the semi-Arians—continued to fight, and the bishops again had to reaffirm the Nicene Creed at the ecumenical Council of Ephesus in 431.

In other words, in the end the early Christians unmistakably decided that Arianism was a very bad idea. The Arian Jesus was not the real Jesus. A Christian cannot be an Arian. An Arian was a heretic—which is to say, someone who firmly rejects the Church's description of the real Jesus—and therefore in great danger of going to hell himself and of taking others there with him.

Now for the experiment: If one Sunday your pastor preached a sermon straight from Arius' writings, treating Jesus as God's creation, would you: (a) know it; (b) object; and (c) find anyone else to join you in objecting?

Most of you will have to say no to the first two questions. Those who can say yes to them will almost certainly have to say no to the third. Yet the early Christians would have known it, would have objected very loudly indeed, and would have found many others (perhaps the whole parish) joining them. It was a very different world.

Why Bother?

I sense a certain irritated squirming in your chair. Why, you may be thinking, would they have consigned someone to hell just because he talked about Jesus in a different way from the majority?

Why would they have hounded a successful evangelist (in how many bars today do you hear Christian doctrine being sung with enthusiasm?) and kept Christians upset for decades? Isn't it more important just to love the Lord and your neighbor as yourself and get on with your life?

There's too much to do, you might continue, to spend time on issues as insignificant as the way the Son related to the Father before time began. If Arius and Alexander both think Jesus is the Savior, don't sweat the details. Christians are divided enough as it is without giving them more reasons to stop speaking to each other.

How can you start a soup kitchen if you're arguing a fine point of theology with the people down at First Arian who own the pots and pans? How can you tell strangers the Lord loves them when you won't hold the ecumenical Good Friday service with the pastor of St. Arius next door?

And anyway, you may well add, we can't put God in a box. Any way of talking about him is so much less than the truth, one sincere effort is pretty much as good as another. Why worry about a few words when you all love the Lord? You shouldn't label someone a heretic and expel him from the Church just because he talks about Jesus differently from the way you do. Isn't the Inquisition over? Haven't we gotten beyond this sort of thing?

And I will say, after a certain irritated squirming in my chair: Yes, we have, and we shouldn't have done it. I cannot stress enough that for the earliest Christians, to know the real Jesus you must say the right things about him, and if you know him, you *will* say the right things about him.

As we shall see, men and women willing to go to the lions for the Lord fought hard for certain teachings—to us, teachings often technical to the point of absurdity—about who he really was. The man with the scars of torture on his body would say that it matters very much what we say about Jesus—indeed, that he bears those scars because he said one thing and not another. For the earliest Christians, getting the words right was a matter of salvation.

Drawing the Real Jesus

This is a simple point, but you must understand it to understand what the early Christians were doing. When they tried so hard to get the words right they were only drawing with words the best picture they could of the real Jesus. A picture drawn with the wrong words might be a very good picture, artistically speaking, but it would not be a picture of Jesus.

They had to draw a picture of a particular man. No other picture would do them any good. No other Jesus could save them. The other Jesuses some people preached might have been fine men that could command a following, but they had the great disadvantage of not existing.

Let me put this another way. A religion of the heart will be a religion of the mind if the heart is faithful and wise. You think about the people you love. When you are away from them, you remember the facts of their lives: how they look, what they think, how they speak, what they do.

And you want to get the facts right. The right facts point to the right person. The wrong facts don't. You can't put someone you love in a box, but you can put him in a picture.

Because the early Christians loved him, they insisted that to know the real Jesus, you must get the words you say about him exactly right. They thought they had the right words because they knew him. They insisted that everyone else get the words right because they wanted others to know him and love him too. They wanted to remember him, and they wanted to make sure they didn't ever remember him wrongly.

In other words, combine knowledge and love, and you get this care for getting the words right that we usually find so weird, if not just silly or rude.

The Way We Think

The early Christians thought very differently from the way we think. We want to be "practical," and think words like "of one essence" impractical. But as we read the early Christians we find that those whose faith was so practical it sometimes got them killed—the Romans wouldn't have bothered killing people whose beliefs made no difference to their lives—assumed that part of being a practical Christian was getting the words right.

Please listen to them as if they might have been right, despite how peculiar their insistence on getting the words right may seem to you. They were closer to the Lord than we are in time and in culture. And they faced death for him.

Give them the deference due those who are our Fathers in the faith and who gave Jesus far greater gifts than we have given him. Don't assume that we know better what the Christian religion ought to be than they did, just because we live sixteen or seventeen centuries later. A people can learn a lot in seventeen hundred years, but they can also forget a lot.

When you are tempted to think we know better than the early Christians, remember which of us bear the scars.

The Mistakes

If you have stopped squirming, let me try to explain further. Perhaps you can see the need for getting the words right by studying some people who got the words wrong and seeing what their mistakes did to our hope of salvation.

Getting the words wrong is what we now call heresy. The one who gets the words wrong is a heretic. This word upsets people nowadays, but all it means is a person who has said something untrue about Jesus, has been warned by the people responsible for such things, and has kept saying it anyway. He may be quite sincere, but he is wrong about something important that he should be getting right. A heretic is, if you will, a traitor.

His Jesus is not the real Jesus, though he may look a lot like the real Jesus. In fact, in the early days the other Jesuses usually looked enough like the real one to fool a lot of sincere people. You could easily give your life to the heretic's Jesus.

You could easily give your life to the heretic's Jesus because the heretic almost always got something right, and usually got right something everyone else had neglected. He could with some reason claim that his version was the real Christianity. Arius demoted Jesus not because he did not like Jesus but because he wanted the Father to be everything God is supposed to be.

The problem with heresy is that whatever the heretic got right, he got right out of context. He insisted on his idea at the cost of other ideas he thought contradicted his. Christianity teaches paradoxes or mysteries that seem like simple contradictions in terms: that God is one and yet three, that Jesus was both God and man.

The heretic solved the problem by saying that one side of the paradox was the truest one, and the other true in a lesser sense. Arius believed that God is three and one, but most truly one, and three in the sense that within that which we call God are two derivative or created deities, the Son and the Holy Spirit.

In other words, the heretic resolved the paradox and released the tension we feel when asked to believe two apparently contradictory things. He almost always did so, as I said, by teaching some truth the orthodox Christians had neglected. This mixture of reformist idealism and simplifying (he would have said clarifying) the teaching gave the heretic's teaching its appeal.

We tend to think of the ancient heresies as if their promoters were like the shabbily dressed men in public parks who hold up badly hand-lettered signs and scream out warnings about alien invasions. They were usually rather charismatic people whose teachings were much more like the urban legends that even normally skeptical people believe because they seem so obviously true.

You will not understand the early Christians until you understand how attractive the mistakes were, and how easy it was to meet a fake Jesus and think he was the real one. Only the real Jesus could save you from hell and bring you to heaven, and that in itself was obviously reason enough to drive out the people who were introducing their victims to a fake Jesus. The more believable was the picture, the more important it was to expose it as a fraud.

I will give three examples of people who got the words wrong, two ancient and one modern. In each, some mistake was made in speaking of the real Jesus, and the result was an idea of our salvation and happiness that offers us much less than the real Jesus will actually deliver.

Gnosticism's Challenge

Consider first one of the Christianized versions of Gnosticism. These Gnostics believed that the real God could not have made a material world, because matter was evil. To say that God created matter would be grossly irreverent. Therefore a sort of lesser god must have created this world.

The real God, however, had to have some connection with this world if we were to have any hope of knowing him, and so the Gnostics argued that he was related to it by layers and layers and layers of beings, rather like companies whose chairman is insulated from the employees by executive vice-presidents and senior vice-presidents and plain vice-presidents and assistant vice-presidents and assistants to the assistant vice-presidents. Many of the Gnostic teachers had an elaborate mythology describing these beings that I find extraordinarily confusing.

As a religion, Gnosticism offered an elaborate system of rituals and ideas, and a special path to salvation offered through a secret knowledge given only to the insiders. (The term "Gnosticism," as you may know, comes from the Greek word for "knowledge.") Gnosticism, as one scholar has put it, is "the sense that the divine is to be discovered by some kind of interior search, and not simply by a savior who is outside you." (You can see why it alarmed people like St. Irenaeus.)

According to this heresy, the human race fell not into sin but into bodies, from the world of spirit to the world of the senses. To be saved, we must learn the Gnostic truths. We are saved, those of us who can be, by escaping the world and ascending to the real God and the purely spiritual world, which is accomplished through an interior search, by being initiated into the Gnostic secrets, and living by the Gnostic rules.

In most Gnostic systems—there were lots—only some men had in them the spark of the real God that let them escape the world. Others were condemned to stay in the bestial material world and disappear at death.

It is hard to know exactly what the Gnostics thought the life of those who ascended back to the real God would be like. They would escape the body and the world of the senses, so the life of the spirit would be a life stripped of much that makes you different from everyone else.

As you would expect, many people tried to Christianize Gnosticism or gnosticize Christianity by working Christ into their system. To do this they had to claim that Scripture—the parts they liked, anyway—was really a Gnostic document. Then they had to explain the inconsistencies between Scripture and Gnostic teachings by claiming to have a secret knowledge that Christ had passed down through the Gnostic brotherhood.

The Scriptures, they would note, described Jesus teaching privately to the disciples the truths he veiled in parables when speaking to the people (Mk 4:34). St. Paul had spoken of truths he shared only with the "mature," which the "natural man" could not understand and in fact thought foolish (1 Cor 2:6, 14-16). This was the knowledge the Gnostics claimed to have.

This secret knowledge, they said, gave the true interpretation of Scripture and revealed its true Gnostic meaning. This gave them an argument almost impossible to argue with. What *do* you say to people who tell you that they see truths you don't see? They always get that superior, patronizing smile that tells you fruitful discussion is now impossible.

The Christianized Gnostics usually made Christ some sort of emissary from the real God who came to bring us a spark of that divine life, so that we could ascend to the real God after him. He appeared in the man Jesus but was not what the ordinary unenlightened Christians crudely thought of as incarnate.

Even among the Christianized Gnostics, only those who were truly "spiritual" could be saved by ascending to the realm of spirit and knowledge. Some of them thought, however, that those who weren't truly spiritual—by which they meant ordinary Christians—could work their way to an inferior sort of salvation. (This was nice of them.)

Gnostic Morals

Gnosticism had, by the way, two very different effects upon morality. If the body was a bad thing to have, you could either try to drive it into submission or you could use it for all the pleasure it could give you, as long as you were careful not to have children and bring more matter into the world. (I won't draw the obvious modern parallel.)

The first seems to be the logical choice for a Gnostic. If the body is a bad thing to have, you should try to use it as little as possible and refrain from enjoying it. And for heaven's sake, don't make more bodies.

Many of them believed, as one Gnostic writer declared flatly, that "marriage and procreation are from Satan." For the Gnostic, to marry was to jump into the traps and illusions of the material world from which you would have trouble freeing yourself. It was rather like taking your first shot of heroin.

However, the second moral position was just as logical a choice for the Gnostic. The Gnostic party animal could justify almost anything he wanted to do by saying that whatever he was doing with his body, his spirit was still free. In fact, that he could use it for pleasure showed how free of it he was.

If he thought himself a Christian he could quote St. Paul's "to the pure all things are pure" (Ti 1:15). One Christian writer reported that the typical Gnostic would use this idea as a pick-up line to seduce women away from their husbands.

However it is that we should balance our subduing of the body with our enjoyment of it, the Gnostic clearly fell off one side or the other. Gnosticism's two moral tendencies would have warned the early Christians against it. The Gnostic gaunt from fasting who refused to marry and thought children an evil, and the drunken Gnostic crawling from brothel to brothel, were alike signs that the religion had made a big mistake at its beginning.

The early Christians were often tempted in the first direction, which helps explain why some liked Gnosticism. For one thing, they tended to share the dominant culture's dislike of the body and its assumption that salvation was purely spiritual.

For another, this Gnostic fear of the body's lures seemed to be apostolic. St. Paul had said that "it is better to marry than to burn" (1 Cor 7:9) and Jesus had announced that in heaven there would no marriage (Mt 22:30). The apostolic writers were always warning their readers against the dangers of the flesh and the world.

But the apostolic writings also affirmed the Hebrew Scriptures that told them God had created the world and called it good, and that he had in effect celebrated the first marriage when he made Eve for Adam (Gn 1:31; 2:21-23). The gospel told them that his Son had performed his first miracle at a wedding (Jn 2:1-11). The apostle Paul had used marriage as a symbol of the Church in his letter to the Christians in Ephesus (Eph 5:25-31). And they had that central scene of a baby lying in a manger (Lk 2:16).

Because the Christians believed all this, they could not think that matter was bad and marriage evil. They may have felt it, but they could not think it. (Unless they rejected the teaching they had been given, thinking they knew better what the body was really like, which of course some did.)

Because the Christian believed that a good God created the body, and had taken a body himself, the Christian could accept what the Gnostic saw rightly—the power of the flesh to control the mind and spirit—and apply the insight safely and wisely. The Christian could teach caution and self-discipline without giving up the pleasures God has given.

The Gnostic impulse could be channeled into a style of Christian spirituality to which some were called but not others. Some would be celibate and others married. Some would live in the deserts half-naked and surviving on crusts of bread, others would live in homes surrounded by their children. Both would subdue their bodies, but in different ways and for different fruit.

Believable Gnosticism

Now, before you laugh at the Gnostic teachings, remember that this all made sense to many people at the time, including Christians. St. John's Gospel spoke of salvation as knowing Christ (Jn 17:3). St. Clement of Alexandria and his brilliant student Origen, two of the formative minds of early Christian history, used Gnostic ideas and language while claiming them for the Church. (Whether or not this was a good idea is something Christians still argue about.)

Gnosticism tried to answer a real philosophical problem: how a God who is perfect and changeless and eternal could have anything to do with a world so flawed and changing as ours. It tried to treat God with reverence when so many religions treated their gods like shopkeepers who were supposed to give them what they wanted in exchange for being worshiped. If the Gnostics put God as far away from man as possible, they did so because they knew that God was very different from us.

Gnosticism offered the hope of salvation and perfection to people who wanted to be saved from their obviously unsatisfactory condition and made perfect. It gave them a way back to God. It also gave a satisfying cosmology—a view of everything—to people who wanted to understand their world, and who hated its religious confusion. It helped them control their bodies, to whose passions they knew they were enslaved.

All this may seem quite strange to us, because our world has erred in the opposite way. Few of us believe that we need to be saved from anything, except perhaps from disappointment that life hasn't turned out the way we expected. Most of us have to do something truly awful before we feel that sense of inner pollution the sensitive people of the ancient world felt almost all the time.

We have little reverence for God. We aren't tempted to put him very, very far away because we don't think about him very much, and a god close enough to be used when we need him is a lot better than one out of hearing. He is like the waiter we want to be standing at the side of the room, where he won't bother us or overhear our conversation but will be over in a second when we summon him.

I am sure many people joined the Gnostics for bad reasons as well. It would have appealed as much to the lusts of the flesh as to the idealism of the heart, and the idealism would have been a good cover for indulging the lusts of the flesh. Think of the hormonally-driven teenagers who insist they have to go to bed with each other because they are in love. Most people are teenagers where God is concerned.

The Gnostic rites in themselves—mysticism with pageantry—must have attracted people, and the desire to be on the inside and to know things your neighbors don't know is an eternal human temptation. Both, by the way, help explain why today Mormon and Mason buildings do not have windows.

And of course the Gnostic system must have appealed greatly to basic human pride, since it taught that your escape from this world to God was your own doing. Irenaeus described one group of Gnostics who believed that they had souls like Christ's and had powers like his. They were so proud of themselves that some of them thought they were better than Jesus because they despised the things in this world more than he did.

But still, in a world that didn't know about the real Jesus, Gnosticism was a religion for the seriously religious. If it seems silly to us, it seems silly for two reasons: We aren't as seriously religious as they were, and we live in a world still formed, even after centuries of secularization, by the belief that God once became man.

The Gnostic Mistake

Gnosticism began with a mistake about creation, but when Christianized, it required a new Jesus. In the Christianized versions of Gnosticism, he couldn't possibly be the Son of God made man, because God would never do such a thing as take a human body. He might put on one as a costume, but only as long as he needed it to share his message with people who were trapped in bodies themselves. He wouldn't be born of a virgin, nor die on a cross, nor rise again in the body.

In the teaching of the Gnostic Cerinthus, for example, Christ entered an extraordinarily good man named Jesus and then left again before he died. Cerinthus flourished about the year 100, and St. Irenaeus thought the apostle John had written his gospel against his teaching.

According to Irenaeus, Cerinthus taught that the world was created by a power not only far from the real God but ignorant of him as well. Jesus had not been born of a virgin but was the biological son of Mary and Joseph. He was, however, "more righteous, prudent, and wise than other men" and at his baptism "Christ descended upon him in the form of a dove from the Supreme Ruler, and then he proclaimed the unknown Father, and performed miracles. But at last Christ departed from Jesus, and then Jesus suffered and rose again, while Christ remained impassible, inasmuch as he was a spiritual being." (Impassible means incapable of suffering.)

This sort of thing, the Christianized Gnostics insisted, was what the Bible was really about. You just had to read it with the right key to realize that its language about creation, incarnation, and resurrection was symbolic and metaphorical. You had to have the key to know what parts to believe, because some of it was simply mistaken. The writers couldn't rise to the spiritual insights needed to see what they should say.

This idea would have attracted some Christians, even if they ought to have known better. It promised them that delicious sense of being on the inside—and as Christians, of being on the inside of the inside. (A good rule for Christians is: Beware a religion with snob appeal.)

More importantly, it made sense to them. The average convert from the religions of the day must have felt some discomfort with that picture of God being a baby (and a Jewish baby, too). A Gnosticized Christianity would, he might easily have thought, let him keep the Jesus he had met and the deep religious sense he had already.

The convert had already gained a superior knowledge and a new insight into Scripture when he joined the Church. He had come to see the world and himself in a radically different way— he had "switched paradigms," as we would say today. It would not be hard to switch one more time, moving in what he thought was the same direction.

Gnostic Salvation

In other words, Gnostic Christianity drew men and women away from the real Jesus. It offered a picture of Jesus that looked enough like him to fool people who didn't know him well enough and might follow the fake Jesus, who would lead them a long way from salvation. It was dangerous.

You see what sort of salvation the Gnostics offered you: peace after the trials of life, through an escape from being trapped in matter into an immaterial and impersonal existence—in effect, the extinction of you as you. You were not redeemed by a God who had taken your place, through your repenting of sins and growing in goodness. You escaped this world by learning the secrets, *if* you were one of the spiritual elite. If you weren't, you died in the trap.

The Christian Gnostic followed this fake Jesus right out of the world of the body and the senses. Gone for the Gnostic would be hymns such as "Silent Night" and "O Sacred Head Sore Wounded" and "Up From the Grave He Arose," which could be sung only by people who (the Gnostic would say) didn't know who Jesus really was.

Some people will find this very attractive. I don't, but many, many people do. "New Age" movements today, and the many forms of westernized Buddhism popular in cities on both coasts and college towns across the country, promise the same sort of thing. The truly spiritual person rises above the affairs of this tawdry, messy world to be merged at last with all other beings in the impersonal spiritual unity of the cosmos.

It is peace, but at the cost of personality. I find much more compelling a salvation in which I remain me, but become the perfect me, in fellowship with all others—family, friends, neighbors, and millions and millions of others drawn from every race and tribe and nation who are (to adapt a phrase from Will Rogers) family I haven't met. In the truly Christian Christ, all of these human beings become perfectly—delightfully, beautifully, compellingly—themselves. They become more themselves the closer they grow to God.

You can get a picture of this growth in C.S. Lewis' book *The Great Divorce,* where those who have just arrived in heaven are almost transparent and can't walk on the grass because it hurts their soft feet. They are barely real because they are not very good. Only those who let go of the besetting sin that has warped their life and personality can be truly themselves enough to enjoy heaven and grow more real as they draw nearer to God.

This salvation is available to everyone who opens his heart to the Lord Jesus Christ. God plays no favorites. I much enjoy the fact that a country priest who kept botching his Latin like the Curé d'Ars, and a simple, sickly young woman like St. Thérèse of Lisieux, and a cantankerous hermit like St. Jerome can all be saints, on the same terms as cardinals and reverend professors of divinity.

Of course, it doesn't matter whether or not you like the Gnostic idea of salvation. Christianity tells you it isn't on offer. You have a body and you have to keep it. You cannot escape your body, though you can be redeemed in the body.

Picture Salvation

Gnosticism promises a sort of extinction. Picture to yourself what the Christian promise of salvation means. It means that heaven can include Uncle Charlie with his joy but without his lust and gluttony, and Aunt Betty with her compassion but without her fear and anxiety, and your friend Mark with his wit but without his cruelty and condescension.

And you as well, without all those ingrown sins that have made you and others unhappy (most of which you don't know about) but with your gifts (most of which you don't know about either) fully developed. It means that you will no longer be a prime example of St. Paul's saying that the good he wants to do he doesn't do, and the evil he doesn't want to do, he does anyway (Rom 7:15). It means that you will be like Christ.

The heaven the real Jesus promises will be a lot more fun than the absorption into the purely spiritual realm that Gnosticism promised. He points us to the Creator and to the goodness of creation, and promises a future that is not escape but redemption.

Jesus said that the kingdom of heaven was like a party (Mt 22:1-14). His enemies thought that he was unspiritual—they accused him of being a heavy drinker (Lk 7:34) and the like—but he meant something like this: When God redeems his creatures, they have the fellowship in joy and praise that the laughter and cheer of a human party point to.

Gnosticism leads to the loss of personality as you are absorbed into the spiritual world. Christianity gives you more personality than you knew you had. The saints, as Dante saw, grew into mountains.

Gnosticism leads to the silence of eternity. Christianity leads to an eternal pleasure and joy and celebration for which the best human party is only the weakest of metaphors.

I hope this begins to explain why the early Christians cared so much to get the words right. If Jesus is the way that we come to the Father and find eternal happiness, we need to know exactly who he is. We don't want to go the wrong way by following the wrong Jesus. What we say about Jesus has vast and everlasting effects on human happiness.

The Case of Marcion

The second case of heretical teaching we will examine is that of Marcion, the most prominent of those who separated the God of Jesus from the creator God and proposed instead what he thought was the true Christianity. He arrived in Rome about 140, was excommunicated in 144, set up his own church (he was quite wealthy), and died about 160.

Marcion did not seem to care for the Gnostics' mythology, but like them he taught that the God of the Scriptures (meaning what we call the Old Testament) was a lesser god or what the Greeks called a "demiurge." This lesser god was a god of law who had no relation to the God of love and grace revealed in Jesus Christ.

Marcion said that the God of the Hebrew Scriptures is "the author of evils," who loved war, didn't know what he wanted to do, and contradicted himself. He was not, in other words, a very good god. But fortunately (I am quoting St. Irenaeus' summary), "Jesus, being derived from that Father who is above the God that made the world ... was manifested in the form of a man to those who were in Judea, abolishing the Prophets and the Law, and all the works of that God who made the world."

Marcion thought that he was revealing the true meaning of the Scriptures and giving due reverence to the true God, the God of Jesus, whom the Law and the Prophets had replaced with their inferior creator god. Jesus said that a good tree could not produce evil fruit (Lk 6:43-44), and here was a god plainly producing evil fruit by the bushel.

Jesus himself was either the true God or his emissary, who condescended to help the poor people bewitched and entrapped by the creator god. He gave his soul for all the souls the creator god had taken, but being from the true God, he couldn't be held in death himself. While temporarily dead, he freed all the souls in Hades. He then ascended back to the true God.

The scholars are not sure quite what Marcion thought about Jesus. He seems to have thought that Jesus assumed a body while he was on earth, but wasn't truly incarnate. Whatever he did, Jesus saved us by showing us the way, not by taking our sins upon himself.

For Marcion, Jesus liberated us from all the Scripture's teaching about law and justice. Unfortunately, the creator god tricked most of the apostolic writers, who mixed up Jesus' message with the teaching of the Hebrew Scriptures. Their works had to be discarded. This left Marcion with his own versions of the Gospel of Luke and ten of St. Paul's letters (all but the pastoral epistles, which he may not have known about). He took out of Luke the story of Jesus' birth and edited the rest of the book and Paul's letters as needed to fit his ideas.

In Marcion's teaching, only the souls who had learned his doctrine would be saved, but their bodies, being earthly, would not share in salvation. Because Marcion held the body and the material world in such contempt, his rules were not, as we say today, "life-affirming." He believed marriage, for example, to be "nothing else than corruption and fornication." Though Marcion preached a God of love, he seems also to have required of his followers a strict morality.

Believable Marcion

Marcion's teaching may look as odd to us as Gnosticism. It is hard to understand why any Christian would have listened to a man who tossed out the entire Old Testament and a good bit of the New and then rewrote what he kept.

At the time, Marcion offered a way to read Scripture that must have looked to many as good a way as the one the Church taught. To the new convert, the Old Testament must have been a very troublesome book. Some Roman Christians may also have liked Marcion's rejection of Jews and Judaism.

The convert had been told the story of God becoming man and dying for his sins, yet here was an inspired book that talked about babies being smashed against rocks (Is 13:16). He had been told that God was a God of grace, yet here was an inspired book with pages upon pages of laws, some of them quite peculiar. He would have heard his teachers finding in the Hebrew Scriptures Christian meanings that on the surface didn't seem to be there at all.

At the time Marcion flourished, most Christians would not

have given him very clear answers to his questions. It took some time to work out how they could understand the Old Testament in a Christian sense. They did so by a way of reading it that found in every passage—even the most unlikely—a Christian meaning.

The Church knew that Jesus fulfilled the Scriptures, and that nothing in the apostolic writings contradicted anything in them, but it hadn't yet answered all the questions people would ask. Many would naturally have settled for Marcion's simpler and clearer answer.

Marcion's teaching had a true religious appeal as well. He proclaimed that God will save us, even though he has no responsibility for us. Marcion offered both an escape from the law and an answer to the problems of reading the Scriptures as if they were God's Word. Like the Gnostics, he also promised relief from the pains of this world in a wonderful heaven in which we'll no longer be held down in suffering by our bodies.

Marcion's Heaven

This religious system appeals to me no more than Gnosticism. But although you will not find any Marcionite churches today, many people still think like Marcion. Any reader who comes to the Scriptures afresh will find the Old Testament a problem and will be vexed by the apparent contradiction between the preaching of God's grace and its demanding moral teaching. And the lure of a faith without any idea of law is always very strong.

As the Gnostics did, Marcion made a mistake about God and creation, which led directly to a mistake about Jesus. As a mistake about Jesus, it was also a mistake about salvation. Marcion's mistake left him with an idea of salvation very different from the Christian one.

This idea had the problem of legalism that unexpectedly seems to come with religions of love without law. I suppose this happens because they have to provide rules to show their followers how to love. Though preaching a God of love, he gave his followers a set of ideas and rules they had to follow if they were to escape the creator God and make their way to the real God revealed in Jesus.

But there was a subtler problem with Marcion's mistake. In *Against Heresies* St. Irenaeus showed that by rejecting the Creator God of the Old Testament Marcion had in fact rejected Jesus as well. If you say no to God the Creator, you say no to his prophet Isaiah, and thus you say no to the Savior prophesied by Isaiah.

Marcion's view of God and Jesus, said Irenaeus, was "the most daring blasphemy against him who is proclaimed as God by the Law and the Prophets." It tears Jesus away from the God we know to be his Father. The Jesus who is not the Son of the Creator is not the real Jesus. If he is not the real Jesus, he is not the Jesus who can save us.

I hope this example also helps to explain why the early Christians cared so much to get the words right. Making up a fake Jesus is easy to do, and finding people who will follow your Jesus is just as easy. The early Christians demanded the real Jesus for the simple reason that they wanted people to be saved.

A Modern Example

The early Christians knew Gnosticism and Marcionism were bad ideas, appealing as they were. They knew they were bad ideas because they knew Jesus and knew the Gnostic and Marcionite Jesuses were frauds. That they got the words right saved them from accepting what must sometimes have seemed to be the sensible answer.

Now let me give you a modern example, where the mistake may be a little harder to see, because it is taught in more modern language. John Macquarrie is one of the leading theologians in England, and his book *The Principles of Christian Theology* has been a basic textbook in seminaries of all sorts, Catholic and Protestant, for over three decades.

He retired a few years ago from a prestigious chair of divinity (the old word for theology) at Oxford University. He is enormously learned. A Catholic-minded Anglican, he has written movingly on his devotion to Mary and to the Blessed Sacrament.

In *Principles*, Macquarrie described the Christian idea as "the old idea that the cosmic process is to be understood as centering in God's dealings with man, in the sacred biblical history of Creation, Fall, redemption, and final consummation." This, he said, is all "pathetically improbable." (He is not all that clear whether he means "pathetically improbable but true" or "pathetically improbable and almost certainly untrue," but he seems to mean the latter.)

The modern man and woman, he believes, can't transpose "the history of Jesus into a mythological framework where he was seen as a supernatural preexistent being who had come down from heaven." This being the case, we must reinterpret the ancient doctrines in ways modern man can accept. To do this Macquarrie uses the philosophical language of "Being."

The Incarnation "is to be understood as the union of a being with Being in the fullest and most intimate way possible." Because Jesus gave up so much for others, and finally died for them, he is for us the "focus of being." To "claim that in Jesus 'the Word became flesh' is to assert that in and through this particular being, Being has found signal expression."

The Child lying in a manger who is nevertheless the One through whom all things were made is, properly understood, a "focus of being." To say that for us men and for our salvation the Son of God came down from heaven is only an ancient way of saying that in this man Jesus we have a "signal expression" of Being.

Not surprisingly, we look to Jesus because he showed us how to live, not because he died on the cross for our sins and rose again. For Macquarrie, the empty tomb is an example of "the usual mythologizing tendency." He means that what he has put in the language of "being," most people must express in stories and pictures, but the wise man will see through these stories and not be so naive as to believe they actually happened.

Salvation, therefore, is knowing the truth revealed in the union of Jesus with Being, that we are united to Being and moving toward a "gathering up of all beings in God." This gathering up is what Christians have pictured as heaven.

Macquarrie's Salvation

Before you laugh, remember that this kind of talk has made sense to many intelligent people and was proposed by a man with a love for Mary and for the sacraments. It is a game attempt to put the Christian idea into words that (Macquarrie thinks) modern people will understand better, accepting what (he thinks) modern science has found to be true, and eliminating the mythological framework that (he thinks) people cannot believe any more.

I can understand some people liking the idea of replacing the Word become flesh with a signal expression of Being, but I don't find it very compelling. I know what Macquarrie is trying to do. He is trying to rescue a Christianity he believes is becoming irrelevant by finding a new way to tell people what it really means. He does it knowing both the tradition and modern philosophy as well as anyone.

I myself would much rather believe that the myths are true, that "myth became fact," as C.S. Lewis put it. I do not see any good reason to believe that in Jesus myth did not become fact. You may claim that all the old words are no good anymore, but the claim is no more plausible than the claim that they are as good as ever.

Many modern people do not believe the old words, but the question to be asked is whether they cannot believe them or will not believe them. If some truly cannot believe them, the question then to be asked is how the old words can be explained till they can.

In this, the old words and the events they point to are much more useful than Macquarrie's *Principles*. A skeptical college student may be driven to prayer by a vision that the Child in a manger created the universe, and that God so loved the world that he sent it his only Son, but he is not likely even to show up at the youth group meeting just because someone said that Jesus is the focus of being.

I think most people would agree. A fact, you can deal with; a philosophical abstraction, you can't. We can decide to follow that Child in a manger or go our own way. We can trust him to bring us to heaven or we can try to get there ourselves, or we can even conclude that there isn't such a place. But we can't do much with a "focus of being."

The language of "Being" is a useful way for philosophers to talk, but it is not a language for religion, which needs realities. As Venerable John Henry Newman wrote, "Many a man will live and die upon a dogma; no man will be a martyr for a conclusion."

Look where Macquarrie's mistakes get us. As with Gnosticism, and for a similar reason, out go "Silent Night" and "O Sacred Head Sore Wounded" and "Up From the Grave He Arose." Macquarrie has replaced the Christian conviction that at one point in human history you could have touched God, and the promise that at the end of history you will be able to do so again, with a vision of experiencing "focused being" that is distinctively vaporous.

Attractive Heresies

This examination of people who taught a Jesus who didn't (and doesn't) exist begins, I hope, to explain why the early Christians were so eager to get right the words they used to speak of Jesus, even when saying them might get them killed. They were talking about their Savior.

If you got the words wrong, men and women would misunderstand, and perhaps even miss, the real Jesus and the salvation he promised. If you got the words wrong, you might not meet the real Jesus at all. You might find yourself following the Gnostic Jesus or the Marcionite Jesus or the focus-of-being Jesus, and those Jesuses couldn't bring you to heaven. They don't exist.

The mistakes of Gnosticism and Marcionism are easy for us to see, and they seem to have been easy for faithful Christians of that day to recognize as well. These Christians were equally rigorous—many today would say "rigid"—in rejecting far more subtle mistakes. For them, in Christian teaching a miss is as good as a mile.

All that said, do not be too quick to condemn early Christians who fell into the errors of their day. Pride goes before a fall, as Proverbs 16:18 tells us and experience regularly confirms. Until we know how attractive and how believable a mistake can be, we can easily fall into the errors of our own day.

The mistakes we have described were not obviously foolish ideas that only the gullible or wicked could ever accept. They certainly could attract men and women for the wrong reasons—the snob appeal of Gnosticism is a good example—but they also appealed to genuine religious impulses and desires. When you think of a Gnostic seeking his way out of this world and into the spiritual world, studying intensely the elaborate mythology of his group in the hope of finding the key to deliverance, remember: There but for the grace of God go you.

Having said that, we ought to remember that the Christianized Gnostics and the Marcionites also took upon themselves the responsibility of deciding what Christians should believe. They may not have meant to, but they looked to the Church not as a mother and teacher but as a cafeteria. Given the freedom to pick and choose, almost anyone will go wrong in what he chooses and what he leaves on the counter.

If you give a starving glutton a credit card and send him to a cafeteria run by gourmet cooks, he may pick out only the healthy foods, but he will be more likely to grab everything he wants. In the spiritual cafeteria, however, much of the food is poisoned. It all looks good, but it's not all good for you, and some of the foods that will do you the most harm look the best.

No Lone Rangers

The early Christians would have told you that you could not design your own Christianity. Pope St. Leo the Great, writing at the end of our period, told of a monk in Constantinople named Eutyches who denied that Jesus truly shared our humanity. This pope's letter well expresses the early Christians' view.

Eutyches was "very unwary and exceedingly ignorant," Leo wrote, and "he refused to understand so as to do well." Worse, he held "blasphemous opinions, and did not give way to those who are wiser and more learned than himself." Now, Leo said, this is what happens to people who find some difficulty in Scripture yet do not look to the prophets or the apostles or the Gospel for an answer, but try instead to figure it out themselves. These people stand out as masters of error because they were never disciples of truth. For what learning has he acquired about the pages of the New and Old Testament, who has not even grasped the rudiments of the Creed? And that which, throughout the world, is professed by the mouth of every one who is to be born again, is not yet taken in by the heart of this old man.

Eutyches was what we would call a lone ranger. He did not understand who Jesus is and would not submit his thinking to those wiser and more learned than he was and to the Creed that contained the truth of the matter. In his independence he became a blasphemer, and blasphemers are not people likely to see the Lord.

This danger wasn't faced by the wise among the early Christians, because they did not think that the truth was theirs to pick and choose. Knowing the real Jesus did not allow for lone rangers, since lots of other people knew him better than they did and had passed on their knowledge.

The early Christians knew there were many questions still to be answered and many problems still to be solved, but it was not their job to answer or solve them. They loved the Church as the place where the answers were to be found even if those answers had not yet been spoken.

The Dean Again

All this the Oxford dean did not see when he told Fr. Brown, "For forms of faith let graceless zealots fight; he can't be wrong whose life is in the right." Those graceless zealots included St. Irenaeus, and St. Justin Martyr, and St. Leo, and a host of others whose lives were in the right—some whose lives were so deeply in the right that the world killed them.

Fr. Brown, with the mind of the early Christian, replied that the dean's slogan was wrong. "How can his life be right, if his whole view of life be wrong? That's a modern muddle that arose because people didn't know how much views of life can differ. Baptists and Methodists knew they didn't differ much in morality; but then they didn't differ very much in religion or philosophy."

The case changed, he continued, "when you pass from the Baptists to the Anabaptists; or from the theosophists to the Thugs. Heresy always does affect morality, if it's heretical enough. I suppose a man may honestly believe that thieving isn't wrong. But what's the good of saying that he honestly believes in dishonesty?"

Like the dean, we tend to separate a religion of the life from a religion of the mind, and most of us think the first much more important than the second. In fact, we often assume that we can't have the first if we have too much of the second.

We assume that even if we do not care to get the words we say about him right, we will still know the real Jesus. I will try to show in the next three chapters that in this matter, we go wrong and the early Christians didn't.

THREE

LOVING THE RIGHT WORDS

The early Christians insisted so fiercely on getting the words they said about Jesus exactly right because they knew him. Of course, he wasn't there at the moment, exactly, having ascended to his Father with the promise that he would come back. They couldn't tug on his sleeve and ask him questions the way the apostles had.

They knew him, nevertheless. They had received his Holy Spirit, who was leading them into all truth and making the Lord present to them. They had the sacraments he'd given them, especially the Eucharist, which St. Ignatius called "the medicine of immortality, and the antidote which prevents us from dying, a cleansing remedy driving away evil, that we should live in God through Jesus Christ."

And they had the stories about Jesus the apostles had taught them. They had four biographies, all long enough and different enough to show them who Jesus was in some detail. Even the apostles' instructions about living the Christian life told them something about Jesus, by showing them how people who knew and loved him would live.

As I said in the last chapter, when the early Christians got the words right they were only drawing in words a good picture of the real Jesus. They wanted to say the right words because they loved him. They thought they had the right words because they knew him. They insisted that everyone else get the words right because they wanted others to know him and love him too. The right words helped them remember him, and helped others to meet him, and made sure they did not ever remember him wrongly.

A Passion for the Right Word

In this chapter we will look at the places in the life and the writings of the early Christians where we would expect to find this passion for getting the words right. We will also look at the places in their lives and writings in which we find this passion where we would *not* expect it.

Note, as we go along, how differently they thought about all this from the way we do. It is a general rule, that where we would not speak the words at all, the early Christians spoke them, and where we would speak just a few words, they spoke a lot of them.

In the early Christians we find this urge to speak exactly the right words about Jesus where we would expect to find it, but even in such places we often find much more of it than we expected. We find the early Christians asking for a Rembrandt where we would settle for connect-the-dots.

Some people write as if the early Christians did not care about getting the words right until some people made such a hash of the teaching that they finally had to put it in writing. They often imply that putting the faith into words was a tragic necessity. This is not true.

It is true that people making a hash of the teaching forced the early Christians to think through many of the fine points, particularly how the truths they knew related to one another (how, for example, the Father could be God and the Son just as much God as the Father, without their being two Gods). It is also true that the bishops, speaking as guardians of the faith, did not make up an official, formal, binding statement of what Christians believed (what we think of as a creed) for over two hundred years, until the Council of Nicaea in the early fourth century.

But it is also true that the early Christians kept the right words from the very beginning. They did not need a challenge to put the faith into words. They still drew slightly different pictures, but they all drew accurate pictures of the same man, much as the four Gospels had told his story in four different ways.

In the second and third centuries, the right words included many different wordings. By "the right words" I do not mean that they spoke of Jesus in exactly the same way, but that they were all speaking accurately of the same man.

Rule of Faith

The first place we find the early Christians insisting on getting the words right was the summaries of the faith they created by the dozen.

The early Christians held to what is usually called the Rule of Faith, an informal statement of the facts of the apostolic teaching laid out in a Trinitarian form and passed on from teacher to teacher. It was, in St. Athanasius' summary, "the actual original tradition, teaching, and faith of the Catholic Church, which the Lord bestowed, the apostles proclaimed, and the Fathers safe-guarded."

Even the earliest of the early Christians believed they knew how to speak of Jesus in some detail and with confidence that they were speaking of the real Jesus. St. Ignatius, for example, warned the Ephesian church not to be fooled by false teaching because "we have received the knowledge of God, which is Jesus Christ ... the gift which the Lord has of a truth sent to us." (His letter to the church in Smyrna opens with a statement of the Rule of Faith.) St. Polycarp had spoken of "the word which has been handed down to us from the beginning."

A few decades later, about the year 180, St. Irenaeus called this informal statement "the rule of truth" and "the preaching" and in one place "the rule of our faith, and the foundation of the building, and the stability of our conversation." He insisted on this Rule partly, as you will remember, because he was writing against people who claimed to have a secret knowledge of what Christianity really was.

Writing just a couple of decades later, the African theologian Tertullian called this informal and unofficial but binding set of truths the "Rule of Faith." (The passage in which he asserts this rule contains his famous questions "What indeed has Athens to do with Jerusalem? What concord is there between the Academy and the Church?" His answer was: Nothing. He was wrong, by the way.)

Irenaeus' and Tertullian's lists of the essential Christian teachings are good ones to use as examples. Irenaeus described the faith the Church had received from the apostles as the belief in one God, the Father Almighty, Maker of heaven, and earth, and the sea, and all things that are in them; and in one Christ Jesus, the Son of God, who became incarnate for our salvation; and in the Holy Spirit, who proclaimed through the prophets the dispensations of God, and the advents, and the birth from a virgin, and the passion, and the resurrection from the dead, and the Ascension into heaven in the flesh of the beloved Christ Jesus, our Lord, and His [future] manifestation from heaven in the glory of the Father to gather all things in one, and to raise up anew all flesh of the whole human race, in order that to Christ Jesus, our Lord, and God, and Savior, and King, according to the will of the invisible Father, "every knee should bow, of things in heaven, and things in earth, and things under the earth, and that every tongue should confess" to Him [Phil 2:10-11] ...

(This is not quite all. Irenaeus finished with a statement about Jesus' judging the wicked and giving immortality to the repentant.)

Tertullian's version is even closer in form to the creed we know. The faith we defend, he wrote, requires the belief that

there is one only God, and that he is none other than the Creator of the world, who produced all things out of nothing through his own Word, first of all sent forth; that this Word is called his Son, and, under the name of God, was seen "in diverse manners" by the patriarchs, heard at all times in the prophets, at last brought down by the Spirit and power of the Father into the Virgin Mary, was made flesh in her womb, and, being born of her, went forth as Jesus Christ; thenceforth he preached the new law and the new promise of the kingdom of heaven, worked miracles; having been crucified, he rose again the third day; having ascended into the heavens, he sat at the right hand of the Father; sent instead of himself the power of the Holy Ghost to lead such as believe; will come with glory to take the saints to the enjoyment of everlasting life and of the heavenly promises, and to condemn the wicked to everlasting fire, after the resurrection of both these classes shall have happened, together with the restoration of their flesh.

"This rule," he concluded, "was taught by Christ."

Writing a few decades later, Origen gave in his *On First Principles* a list of truths beginning with God the Father and ending with angels, "clearly delivered in the teaching of the apostles." Even those he called "somewhat dull in the investigation of divine knowledge" could understand and hold this teaching without any trouble or confusion.

Even over a hundred years later, near the end of the fourth century, St. Gregory of Nyssa could still settle an argument against an Arian bishop by appealing to the Rule. It is proof enough, he said, "that the tradition has come down to us from our fathers, handed on, like some inheritance, by succession from the apostles and the saints who came after them."

"Who," he continued, "is so foolish and so brutish as to account the teaching of the evangelists and apostles, and of those who have successively shone like lights in the churches, of less force than this undemonstrated nonsense?" (By "brutish," he meant "like an animal." Today we might say "harebrained.")

Drawing From the Bank

The early Christians believed that the apostles had given them this Rule of Faith, and that the Holy Spirit had delivered it safely to them. God gave the knowledge of the real Jesus to those who knew him. "God himself has sent from heaven and placed among men the truth, the holy and incomprehensible Word, and has firmly established him in their hearts," in the words of the *Epistle to Diognetus*, an evangelistic letter probably written in the middle of the second century.

They knew the Rule because they'd listened closely to those who knew the Rule. St. Irenaeus himself told of sitting at the feet of St. Polycarp as he'd related what he'd heard from St. John and others who had known the Lord. "These things being told me by the mercy of God, I listened to them attentively, noting them down, not on paper but in my heart," he wrote. "And continually, through God's grace, I recall them faithfully."

The Church could give you the truth, Irenaeus claimed, "since the apostles, like a rich man [depositing his money] in a bank, lodged in her hands most copiously all things pertaining to the truth: so that every man, whosoever will, can draw from her the water of life. For she is the entrance to life; all others are thieves and robbers."

Though scattered throughout the world, the early Christians carefully preserved the faith they'd received as if they lived in one house, Irenaeus said. The Church believed these teachings

just as if she had but one soul, and one and the same heart, and she proclaims them, and teaches them, and hands them down, with perfect harmony, as if she possessed only one mouth. For, although the languages of the world are dissimilar, yet the import of the tradition is one and the same.

The churches all over the world, from Germany, Spain, and Gaul to Egypt, Libya, and Palestine, all believe and hand down the same teaching. Just "as the sun, that creature of God, is one and the same throughout the whole world, so also the preaching of the truth shines everywhere, and enlightens all men that are willing to come to a knowledge of the truth."

If Christians disagree about the faith, he said, they ought to look to "the most ancient churches with which the apostles held constant intercourse, and learn from them what is certain and clear." Even if the apostles had not left their writings, Christians would have been able confidently "to follow the course of the tradition which they handed down to those to whom they did commit the Churches."

So confident were they in the Rule of Faith that they believed it brought salvation even to those who had no knowledge of the Scriptures. The Christian barbarians, Irenaeus wrote, have "salvation written in their hearts by the Spirit, without paper or ink, and carefully preserve the ancient tradition." They didn't know Greek or Latin, but in their teaching and the way they lived "they were very wise indeed because they had the faith, and they pleased God."

Even without the Scriptures, the barbarians would know an error when they saw one. If anyone preached to them a false Jesus, they would clap their hands over their ears and run as far away as possible. They wouldn't even listen, because "by means of that ancient tradition of the apostles, they do not let themselves even think anything taught by these teachers, among whom neither Church nor doctrine has ever been established."

The Rule of Faith, in fact, taught the early Christians what Scripture said. (We'll look at this in more detail in chapter five.)

When you are learning the faith, St. Cyril of Jerusalem told the people he was preparing for baptism, "keep only that which is now delivered to you by the Church, and which has been built up strongly out of all the Scriptures." He told them to memorize the creed he taught them, but to expect that later, "at the proper season," they would find that each claim in the creed could be confirmed from Scripture.

> For the articles of the faith were not composed as seemed good to men; but the most important points collected out of all the Scripture make up one complete teaching of the faith. And just as the mustard seed in one small grain contains many branches, so also this faith has embraced in few words all the knowledge of godliness in the Old and New Testaments. Take heed then, brethren, and "hold fast the traditions which you now receive, and write them on the table of your heart."

Beyond the Pale

Some modern writers have claimed that a Christian couldn't be wrong until the position he held had been officially defined and condemned. No one was wrong about Jesus, for example, until the first Council of Nicaea in 325 began to define what Christians believed and what they didn't.

This is not true. The early Christians knew the real Jesus and expected each other to know him too. Remember that Archbishop Alexander had no problem excommunicating Arius. Those outside the Church and its Rule of Faith "are beyond the pale of the truth," St. Irenaeus warned. (A pale is the area inside a fence, marking off those who belong from those who don't.)

Whoever refuses the Rule of Faith the apostles had left, he continued, "despises the companions of the Lord; nay more, he despises Christ himself the Lord; yea, he despises the Father also. He stands self-condemned, resisting and opposing his own salvation, as is the case with all heretics."

They will someday rise from the dead and have to admit that Jesus is Lord, but at that point it won't do them any good. Those who "rise up in opposition to the truth, and exhort others against the Church of God, [shall] remain among those in hell."

In the same way that someone "drugged by Circe [would] become a beast," declared St. Clement of Alexandria, anyone who "spurned the ecclesiastical tradition, and darted off to the opinions of heretical men, has ceased to be a man of God and to remain faithful to the Lord. But he who has returned from this deception, on hearing the Scriptures, and turned his life to the truth, is, as it were, from being a man made a god."

In his battle with those who denied that the Holy Spirit is equal with the Father and the Son, St. Basil said his opponents' real target was the faith.

The one aim of the whole band of opponents and enemies of sound doctrine is to shake down the foundation of the

faith of Christ by leveling apostolic tradition with the
ground, and utterly destroying it.... They clamor for written proof, and reject as worthless the unwritten tradition
of the Fathers.

Those who will not accept the unwritten tradition "make their
own blasphemy more authoritative than the law prescribed by
the Lord."

Loving the Story

As I just said, many scholars have described the development of
Christian teaching as if no one cared about getting the words
right until they needed the right words to put down an error.
They do not see that the early Christians loved the facts of Jesus'
life so much they told them to each other whether or not anyone else was even listening, much less getting the facts wrong.

One of the great modern scholars of Church history has
argued that even in St. Irenaeus' statements of the Rule of Faith
in *Against Heresies,* "the influence of anti-heretical motives is,
on the whole, surprisingly slight." He noted St. Justin Martyr's
writings "reproduce the primitive *kerygma* [what we call "the
Gospel"], without bending it to any appreciable extent to
polemical or apologetic needs."

What he meant is that the versions of the Rule of Faith the
early Christians gave us weren't directed at the enemy of the
moment. Irenaeus and the others seem to have been giving us
the real Christian teaching, the teaching that Christians shared
among themselves.

This tells us that they loved the story for itself. They didn't suddenly become interested in getting the words right when someone got them wrong. They didn't wait to draw Jesus' picture till someone started posting a bad picture around town. The apostles had given them a very good picture—the image and likeness, you might say—and they loved to look at it, because it was the picture of the real Jesus.

That they loved the story for itself explains why they hated mistakes so much. Mistakes ruined the story. A bad picture did not look like Jesus. It was as if the heretics took the picture of the real Jesus that the early Christians loved to pass around among themselves and drew a mustache on his face and crossed his eyes.

The pictures matter. We don't see this very easily when a picture is drawn with words, as it is in a Rule of Faith or a creed. But we can see it in other ways, because the problem comes up all the time, even today.

In the last few years, southern Americans have divided over the display of the Confederate flag in state buildings. For many white southerners, the flag means a heritage of independence and courage, of their grandparents' working their own land and making a life for their families. For many black southerners, however, the flag means a heritage of oppression, of their great-grandparents chained together in the hold of a ship and then being sold like animals in a market.

A flag flying over a state capitol is not a piece of colored cloth put up as a decoration. It is a symbol. The flag means something very important to people. They fight over it for good reason.

Someone else who does not care about the history cannot tell them all to stop fighting over a mere flag. In the same way, we are wrong to think that the early Christians should not have cared so much for a mere set of words. That set of words—the Rule of Faith—was their flag. It was, in fact, their battle flag.

Droning the Creed

I sense you squirming a little. The only time you meet a statement like the Rule of Faith is when you say the Nicene Creed in church on Sundays, and you've never thought it was something to get that excited about, much less fight over.

Standing up on Sundays and reciting the Nicene Creed has always seemed to you the most boring part of the liturgy. It sticks out from everything else. This dry, plain, intellectual statement doesn't seem to fit in an act of worship. It's a bit like reading the mortgage in the middle of a wedding ceremony. Dramatically speaking, it's a disaster.

Most of us know the feeling. On some Sundays the Scripture lessons and the sermon have either made you uncomfortably aware of your own sins and driven you to beg God for mercy, or they've reminded you of what God has done for you and driven you to praise him for the mercy he has shown you. Scripture and sermon have brought you to feel the truth in a new way. You want to drop to your knees in repentance or stand up and sing praises.

Then, when your heart has been so deeply moved, everyone stands up and drones out this long list of mostly rather abstract statements. Your feelings vanish. They are usually gone by the time everyone is flying through "GodfromGod, lightfromlight, trueGodfromtrueGod."

This is your fault. Just think what you are saying in the words of the Nicene Creed. Everything you have just felt finds its support, its reason, its justification, in the truths you are droning out. It bores you either because you don't yet know the God of whom it speaks—whatever you happen to be feeling—or because you've never learned what the Creed really means.

Think of the Creed as the picture of the Jesus you love, held up before you and the rest of the people for a minute or two. You need to look at it carefully, not glance at it without really seeing it, the way you look at pictures of the "Mona Lisa" in books as you flip the pages.

You will respond to this picture depending on what God is doing in your heart at the moment. If you feel like dropping to your knees to beg his forgiveness, say the Creed as an informal confession, contrasting what it tells you God has done with your own unworthiness. If you feel like standing and singing, say it as a hymn of praise or a love song, thanking the Lord for each fact as you say it.

Evangelism

A second place we find the early Christians insisting on getting the words right is in their attempts to bring others to know the real Jesus. We have very little record of their evangelistic preaching and writing. They didn't leave us much of this sort of thing, because they didn't invite secretaries when they shared the Christian story in public and private. Nor did they speak from manuscripts. They knew what they needed to say and didn't have to write it up before they said it.

I mention this because some writers insist that the early Christians spent too much time fighting over who Jesus really is and too little telling other people about him. They say this, I think, because so many of the early Christian writings we have today are arguments about Jesus.

Many of these writers imply that fighting over who Jesus really is must be a bad thing. It's not "New Testament Christianity." They think the early Christians wanted to get the words right because they were not following the Lord in trust, but instead "freezing" the faith into a set of words in an attempt to make the Christian life easier.

This is not fair to the early Christians. We don't have all the records. We have a lot of the memos they sent to each other, but we don't have many examples of their advertising campaigns and sales pitches. But even reading the memos alone tells us very clearly that they wanted to sell their product. They had to write all these memos only because they had to deal with colleagues and former colleagues who were trying to sell a counterfeit and using the company's name to trick the buyers.

We do have some examples of their evangelistic writing, like the *Epistle to Diognetus,* written in the second century. Here, in a letter intended to bring a man to know the real Jesus, we find this same interest in getting the words right. The unknown writer doesn't just invite his reader to meet Jesus as a modern evangelist might. He doesn't just insist that we need Jesus to save us from our sins as many preachers do today.

Instead, he lays out very carefully who Jesus actually is. Not at great length, mind you, but enough to make clear who the Savior is. He stresses that God did not send to us "any servant or angel or ruler" but "the very creator and fashioner of all things." God sent Jesus as a "king sending his own son who is himself a king. He sent him as God, he sent him as Man to men."

The Father sent his Son, the writer continued, because God "himself took on the burden of our iniquities, he gave his own son as a ransom for us, the holy one for the transgressors, the incorruptible for the corruptible, the immortal for mortals. For what else could cover our sins but his righteousness? In who else was it possible that we, the wicked and ungodly, could be justified, except in the Son of God alone?"

The writer of the *Epistle to Diognetus* wrote like the evangelists of today, but he insisted much more than they do on explaining who Jesus is. He wanted to get the words right because only the real Jesus can save.

The difference between the *Epistle to Diognetus* and a modern evangelistic tract or video may be small, but it's still significant. The modern tract may talk about Jesus and his Father, but almost in passing. Instead, it will typically feature the worldly benefits of conversion. The reader wouldn't realize that Jesus' relation to his Father is the crucial matter, and that unless he has a specific relation there will be no benefits, in this world or the next.

Baptism

A third place in the life of the early Christians where we expect to find them insisting on the right words, but find them insisting on more words than we might expect, is the baptismal rite. At a very early date, anyone who wanted to be baptized was asked to say exactly who he thought the Father and the Son and the Holy Spirit are.

In *The Apostolic Tradition,* a book that tells about worship in Rome in the early third century, St. Hippolytus tells how the converts had to declare their faith before being baptized. We presume that if they gave the wrong answers, they were not baptized.

Each of those to be baptized faced west and renounced Satan. To say the right words about Jesus, you first had to leave behind this world and the prince of this world. You had to defect from the country you grew up in.

Having broken with the devil, the one to be baptized turned to the east and stepped down into the water. (The east is the direction of the sunrise and therefore a symbol of resurrection.) He was asked to declare his belief in the Father, then asked to declare his belief in the Son, and then asked to declare his belief in the Holy Spirit. He was put under the water after each declaration.

The first question Hippolytus recorded was simply, "Do you believe in God the Father Almighty?" But the second was longer:

Do you believe in Christ Jesus, the Son of God, who was born of the Holy Spirit and the Virgin Mary, who was crucified in the days of Pontius Pilate, and died, and rose the third day living from the dead, and ascended into heaven, and sat down at the right hand of the Father, and will come again to judge the living and the dead?

The last question was, "Do you believe in [the] Holy Spirit, in the Holy Church, and the resurrection of the dead?"

You would expect this sort of thing in a baptism. It is a

contract of sorts, and contracts always have conditions. But the Christian contract never has any fine print, because the Church doesn't want anyone coming in who doesn't know what he's getting into.

What might strike us about this early baptismal rite, however, is how many conditions the early Christians included when they didn't have to. In baptism they voluntarily added conditions to the contract they wanted to sign.

Jesus had told his followers to baptize people "in the name of the Father and of the Son and of the Holy Spirit" (Mt 28:19). The early Christians could have used that formula. It was Jesus' formula, after all.

Being simple, it left a lot of "wiggle room," and you never know when you might want to wiggle. But the early Christians didn't want wiggle room. They *wanted* to add more conditions by which to bind themselves. They *liked* adding details, laying out a little more completely the faith to which they were giving their lives.

No Wiggle Room

The early Christians wanted people to be saved. They believed that people must be baptized to be saved. They needed members, being a small, persecuted, and socially eccentric group. Yet they set the requirements for baptism and Church membership high. You had to confess the Christian faith in some detail, at a time when saying so could get you eaten by lions or sent to the galleys or the mines of Sardinia, where you would be worked to death. (You'd take the lions if you had a choice.)

That could easily happen when St. Hippolytus was writing. Getting baptized was a heroic thing to do. Hippolytus reported in *The Apostolic Tradition* the rule that anyone who was getting ready for baptism and was "apprehended for the Name" was not to worry about being killed before he was baptized, because if he was, he would "be justified, having been baptized in his own blood."

Read again the second baptismal question. The one to be baptized was not asked just to confirm his belief in Jesus the Son. He was asked to confirm his belief in the Incarnation of the Son in history—during the tenure of a particular Roman official—as well as that Man's unique relation to the God of the cosmos and his continuing divine authority in our history.

I don't want to push this too far, but the added details all make it much more difficult to treat Christianity as one religious choice among many. They cut out much of the room in which a Christian of that time might well have been tempted to wiggle.

The man who had said only that Jesus is the Son of God could always say later that he meant "the Son" in the sense of "a manifestation," and that he fully understood that other people believed just as sincerely in other manifestations of the divine. Being able to say this might be very useful when a Roman governor gave you the choice of offering a brief prayer to the emperor or being whipped and beaten and then sent to the lions or the galleys.

When you have added to "the Son" all that this baptismal rite added, however, you have made it much harder to deny that Jesus is the only one of his kind. When you have said he sits at the right hand of the Father and will return to judge every man, woman, and child who ever lived, you have pretty much said:

This man Jesus, who lived and died in Palestine a couple of hundred years ago, is God. There are no others. He's it.

And by saying this you have also said: The emperor is not God. And Diana, she's not God, either. And Mithras is no more God than Diana or the emperor. Saying such things could really, really upset your neighbors, not to mention the government, and either one could kill you.

Delivered From Idols

Again, I don't want to push this too far, because we can't know with certainty why such things as baptismal questions developed the way they did. I think, though, that we get some insight into these matters from the general mind of the early Christians, and also from our experience in a similar sort of world. This desire to cut out all the room to maneuver and close all the loopholes seems to have been natural for them. They did it all the time.

It was natural for them, in part, because they did not want people to give up what they had received in baptism. When you were baptized, you not only joined a group of people, you agreed to an extensive set of statements they all insisted were true. You had to accept their picture of the real Jesus. The Church was a community, a body gathered by shared beliefs and commitments, not a club.

As a result, whoever gave up the picture of Jesus he had taken on at his baptism gave up Jesus himself. "After recognizing that this salvation is established through the Father and the Son and the Holy Ghost, shall we fling away 'that form of doctrine' we received?" asked St. Basil the Great in the late fourth century.

The Christian who denied what he had then received was now *further* away from salvation than when he had first received it, Basil said. If you denied what you'd said then about Jesus, you denied Jesus, and you gave up what he did for you. "Whoever does not always and everywhere keep to and hold fast as a sure protection the confession which we recorded at our first admission [at baptism]," he continued,

> when, being delivered from the idols, we came to the living God, constitutes himself a stranger from the promises of God.... Can I then, perverted by these men's seductive words, abandon the tradition which guided me to the light, which bestowed on me the boon of the knowledge of God, whereby I, so long a foe by reason of sin, was made a child of God?

Believing the words the early Christians had gotten exactly right was a "sure protection" against losing the promises of God. Remember what God had promised, as described by St. Peter: that we would become partakers of the divine nature (2 Pt 1:4). Such intimacy with God himself was too good an ending to risk losing by wiggling when you should have stood firm.

It was, in fact, the only happy ending possible for fallen men and women. You can see why they kept cutting out the wiggle room.

Doctrinal Prayers

We have seen several places now where the early Christians went out of their way to say exactly the right things about Jesus, and said more things about him than they needed to. They held an elaborate Rule of Faith; they explained in detail who Jesus is when they told people about him; and they made the entrance rite more complex and binding than they needed to.

We also find them talking about Jesus in this particular way in unexpected places, often when we wouldn't think of speaking about him that way at all. As I said before, please note how differently they thought and acted from the way we do. The differences may often be small—a few words here and there—but I think they tell us a lot.

We find this love for talking about Jesus in detail in some of their prayers, for example. We find it even in prayers offered by Christians who were about to die. Take the prayer offered by the second-century martyr St. Polycarp after he was bound to the pile of wood upon which he would be burnt.

According to the report passed down by his disciples, he began his prayer by setting out exactly who it was to whom he was praying. "O Lord God Almighty, the Father of thy beloved and blessed Son Jesus Christ," he began, in the same way we might begin. But then he added a few more details we would probably leave out, adding "by whom we have received the knowledge of thee, the God of angels and powers, and of every creature, and of the whole race of the righteous who live before thee."

He then thanked God that he'd been counted worthy of martyrdom. He ended the prayer the same way he began it: "I glorify thee, along with the everlasting and heavenly Jesus Christ, thy beloved Son, with whom, to thee, and the Holy Ghost, be glory both now and to all coming ages. Amen."

Think about this prayer. In the same situation, most of us would say something like "God, help!" or "Please put out the fire!" or (the holier among us might say) "Father, I'm coming home." If we prayed at any greater length, it would simply never occur to most of us to begin as Polycarp did, with something so blatantly doctrinal. It wouldn't seem the right moment for intellectual niceties.

Polycarp does not say much, but he says more than we would. Facing death, we might rehearse something of what God has done in history or in our own lives to support the request we are about to make.

We might say, "You saved the Israelites from the Egyptians, so please save me from this robber," but we would not lay out the doctrine of the Trinity. Upon hearing the words "I'm going to kill you" from someone with a large gun, we would not begin to pray, "O Father, Almighty, maker of heaven and earth, of all things, visible and invisible ..."

Flying the Flag

Yet Polycarp's prayer was not as odd as you might think. A martyr was about to die for Jesus and naturally would say something about him. If you're going to die, you want people to know who it is you are dying for.

Put another way, the early Christian martyrs were soldiers marching into battle and wanted to fly the flag. The fourth-century historian Eusebius began his description of their deaths noting that other writers tell about wars fought for family and country. He was going to tell about "the most peaceful wars waged in behalf of the peace of the soul," of "men doing brave deeds for truth rather than country, and for piety rather than dearest friends."

Not all the martyrs prayed like Polycarp, of course, but I am rather sure they all thought like him. Maybe he simply knew how to say what all the others felt and would have said had they the same gifts. At any rate, as a great and early martyr, and one who had known apostles, he is a model for us.

We may think Polycarp's prayer odd because we wouldn't think of saying so much about Jesus in a prayer. The problem with our appreciating such prayers may not be in their irrelevance but in our ignorance. Maybe we ought to learn to say so much about Jesus in our prayers.

Ah, you may say, that was the way they did things then, but it is not relevant now. The ceremonial speech of their day always included a description of the one being addressed, but we don't talk that way. We will write "Dear Dr. Jones," but we will not write "Dear Dr. Jones, greatest of friends of the poor, most generous of benefactors, whose kindness is known to all."

Not exactly. If you think about it, the ceremonial language they used isn't as foreign to us as we may think. As I've said before in different ways, when we speak of and to Jesus, we're speaking of and to Someone we love. We are just as ceremonial as the ancients were when we speak to those we love, in our own, less formal, way.

I know men, for example, who often address their wives as "mother of my children," to celebrate the fact that she is the mother of their children. Saying it obviously gives them pleasure, because the fact that this woman has borne their children is so wonderful. I think this is what Polycarp was doing when he prayed as he did.

To this you may reply that even if I am right, the idea is not all that useful. But I wouldn't say this, were I you. The evidence is against you. The early Christians' love of the Lord worked even in purely human terms. The Church that spoke this way about Jesus, and kept speaking this way even when the rulers tried to kill off its members, kept growing.

"Do you not see them [the Christians] flung to the wild beasts, to make them deny their Lord, and they are yet unconquered?" asked the writer of the *Epistle to Diognetus*. "Do you not see that the more of them that are punished the more their numbers increase? These things look not like the achievements of man. They are the power of God; they are the proofs of his presence."

Nailed to the Cross

The early Christians talked about Jesus in that way when they were about to die, because this was the Jesus for whom they were dying. "He who is near to the sword is near to God; he that is among the wild beasts is in company with God; provided only he be so in the name of Jesus Christ," wrote St. Polycarp's friend St. Ignatius, who went to his own martyrdom in Rome in 107. (It is thought that he gave his life for Christ in the Coliseum, where he may have been eaten by lions.)

Ignatius wrote the Christians in Smyrna that they were "perfected in an immovable faith, as if [they] were nailed to the cross of our Lord Jesus Christ, both in the flesh and in the spirit." Their belief in the real Jesus kept them with him at his cross, as if they were nailed there too, when their chance to suffer for him came. They loved Jesus; therefore they kept the faith. They loved Jesus; therefore they spoke of him in exact words.

Wait, you may be saying, Ignatius was talking about the Christian faith in Jesus Christ, not a particular set of words. Well, yes and no. Let me put it this way: Ignatius was talking about having faith in Jesus, but having faith in Jesus included knowing a lot about him. "The faith" to which the Christians were nailed was a faith in a particular man, about whom they knew a number of very important facts. Christians had to accept the facts for their faith to be true faith in the real Jesus.

They were saved through Jesus' death, but this did not mean they could speak about him however they wished. Ignatius told the Christians in Smyrna that they were "established in love through the blood of Christ, being fully persuaded" that Jesus

> was the Son of God, "the firstborn of every creature," God the Word, the only-begotten Son, and was of the seed of David according to the flesh, by the Virgin Mary; was baptized by John, that all righteousness might be fulfilled by him; that he lived a life of holiness without sin, and was truly, under Pontius Pilate and Herod the tetrarch, nailed [to the cross] for us in his flesh.

You see how Ignatius thought about this. The Jesus who saved us was the One about whom we knew several crucial facts. When you are talking about Jesus, facts are never just facts. Words are never just words.

One scholar remarked on the "dry-as-dust enumeration of facts" in one of the earliest versions of the Rule of Faith, a statement much like this one. Yet those statements would not have been dry to those who were willing to die for them, and who felt that such facts established them in the love of Jesus Christ. Any list of facts is dry reading till you know what they tell you. If they tell you about someone you love, they come alive, because each dry fact points you to the beloved and because together they make a picture you love to look at.

Doctrinal Encouragements

I trust you see my point. The early Christians loved the real Jesus so much that they talked about him all the time. They cared what they said about him, to get the details right and include as many details in the picture as they could manage. We just saw this in the prayer and letters of two martyrs.

We find this same desire to speak about Jesus in another unexpected place: when one early Christian encouraged another. This isn't a major point, but it is another of those places where the early Christians sometimes spoke of Jesus in surprising detail.

As St. Ignatius was traveling to his martyrdom in Rome, he urged St. Polycarp to "stand firm, as does an anvil which is beaten. It is the part of a noble athlete to be wounded, and yet to conquer." After more such encouragement, he told Polycarp to "look for Christ, the Son of God."

This we would expect. An anvil and an athlete are good symbols of perseverance, and of course the Christian must always look to Christ. But Ignatius didn't just give Polycarp this instruction; he gave him a detailed description of the Christ he was supposed to look for. This Christ is he

> who was before time, yet appeared in time; who was invisible by nature, yet visible in the flesh; who was impalpable, and could not be touched, as being without a body, but for our sakes became such [as] might be touched and handled in the body; who was impassible [meaning incapable of suffering] as God, but became passible for our sakes as man; and who in every kind of way suffered for our sakes.

Here Ignatius told Polycarp to look for Christ and then told him what Christ looks like. Jesus' name by itself wasn't enough to ensure that Polycarp got the right man. Ignatius had to fill out the description with important details.

We do not speak this way. We do not think that encouraging our brothers and sisters includes telling them who Jesus is. We would leave out the description, or else only mention whatever Jesus had done that would be most relevant to the friend we were trying to encourage.

Apparent Contradictions

You may have noticed that in the list he gave St. Polycarp, St. Ignatius seemed to be emphasizing the need to hold together the apparently contradictory facts of Jesus' life and person. On the one hand Jesus said, "The Father is greater than I" (Jn 14:28). On the other, he said, "I and the Father are one" (Jn 10:30).

As many people have noted, the clearest sign of a serious theological mistake is that it takes one of these facts and discards the other. The early Christians developed their thoughts on many matters partly to explain the union of apparent contradictions, because to lose the union was to lose the truth. It left you with something unbalanced or misshapen.

The real Jesus was someone no real God and no real man could be, or so the world thought. The early Christian seemed to have been always alert for signs that someone had fallen off the truth on one side or the other. There was a tension in the claim that Jesus was truly God and truly man. The truth wanted to spring apart if you took your hands off both ends, like a tightly wound jack-in-the-box with lids at the top and the bottom.

We may not feel this to be a problem—I must admit I don't—but if I may make the point again, we don't feel the problems as deeply as did the early Christians because we don't feel the truths as deeply as they did. What are stock phrases to us—"God of God" and "of one being with the Father," for example—were to them quite shocking and disturbing claims. I used to feel they went too far, but as I began to learn more I realized that I was simply a dullard.

This difficult tension gives us another reason that they cared so much to get the words exactly right. An Ignatius or a Polycarp or an Irenaeus could hold together two ideas that didn't naturally go together, but they wrote for people likely to drop one or the other when the strain of holding them together became too great. They knew most people would find it easier to say that Jesus was God and not really Man, or Man and not really God, than to say he was just as much one as the other.

For that reason, they demanded that Christians hold without

a single change the words the Church had gotten exactly right. This was the picture of the real Jesus. It wasn't the picture most people would draw, left on their own, and therefore they couldn't be left on their own to draw whatever picture they liked.

I don't think anyone could prove this, but I wonder whether Ignatius offered his description of Jesus as praise, knowing that Polycarp would join in that praise when he read it. It was a fantastic story in the old sense of seeming to come from a fantasy, and in the new sense of being something almost too wonderful to bear.

Doctrinal Instructions

We find this love of saying the right words about Jesus in a third unexpected place: instructions to the clergy. Writing to the priests of Philippi, St. Polycarp told them to serve Jesus "in fear, and with all reverence, even as he himself has commanded us.... Let us be zealous in the pursuit of that which is good, keeping ourselves from causes of offense."

All this we would expect. Of course the clergy should serve the Lord, and work hard, and avoid offending people by behaving badly. But Polycarp did not leave it there. He continued by telling the clergy to keep themselves also "from false brethren, and from those who in hypocrisy bear the name of the Lord, and draw away vain men into error." It was not enough to serve the Lord; they had to avoid those who pretended to serve the Lord but preached someone else.

Look at Polycarp's logic. He told the priests to pursue the good, which led him directly to the need to repel those who pretended to be Christians while speaking the wrong words about Jesus. When he went on to explain what he meant, he began by citing St. John's first letter: "For whosoever does not confess that Jesus Christ has come in the flesh, is antichrist" (1 Jn 4:3).

Then he adds his own charges to John's. Whoever "does not confess the testimony [meaning martyrdom] of the cross, is of the devil; and whosoever perverts the oracles of the Lord to his own lusts, and says that there is neither a resurrection nor a judgment, he is the firstborn of Satan."

The people who said the wrong things about Jesus were doing the devil's work. This explains why the clergy should avoid them. To say wrong words like "the Son of God didn't really die on the cross" or "Jesus didn't rise from the grave" wasn't a mere disagreement among friends or a sincere mistake or an alternative within the diversity of Christian theologies. It was the devil's work.

The remedy he urged upon the priests of Philippi has three parts. First, he told them to "return to the word which has been handed down to us from the beginning." By this he meant not only the apostolic writings but the Rule of Faith. Second, they had to pray intensely and keep fasting. Third, they always had to ask "the all-seeing God 'not to lead us into temptation,' for as the Lord has said: 'The spirit truly is willing, but the flesh is weak.'"

Polycarp was not merely giving advice, he was telling them what to do. His instructions apply to everyone in the priesthood of believers, because every Christian has the job of conveying Jesus to others. We have to be careful that we convey to them the real Jesus, and not any of the devil's substitutes.

Patrick's Confession

We find this unexpected desire to say the right words about Jesus in personal testimonies as well. St. Patrick, the fifth-century Briton missionary to Ireland, wrote the story of his life a few years before he died. Kidnapped as a child and sold into slavery in Ireland, Patrick escaped after a few years and returned home a convinced Christian. A few years later he returned to Ireland to evangelize the island.

In his life's story, called the *Confession,* he barely begins telling the story of his life when he suddenly breaks into a long statement of Christian teaching. He says that he cannot keep silent about what God did for him and then, instead of starting to tell his own story as we expect, says:

> There is no other God, nor ever was, nor will be, than God the Father unbegotten, without beginning, from whom is all beginning, the Lord of the universe, as we have been taught; and his Son Jesus Christ, whom we declare to have always been with the Father, spiritually and ineffably begotten by the Father before the beginning of the world, before all beginning; and by him are made all things visible and invisible.

Patrick goes on at some length (125 more words in the English translation) to describe the Incarnation and the Holy Spirit.

This surprises us, but Patrick explains what he is doing. The sentence before the statement just quoted says: "This we can give to God in return after having been chastened by him, to exalt and praise his wonders before every nation that is anywhere under the heaven." For Patrick, to exalt and praise God's wonders was to tell people who he is.

Think, again, how very different this is from anything most modern Christians would do. Would a modern Christian, even a very conservative one, ever think to start telling the story of his life with the Nicene Creed? How would we react if he did?

Imagine a Christian talk show. The host settles his guest on the couch, then sits on his chair, leans forward, and with a concerned face says, "John, tell us about your life."

"Bob, I'd love to," John says. "You know, Bob, I wasn't much of a Christian as a kid and then I started doing drugs in high school. Jesus saved me from that. But you know what I'd really like to do is just praise the Lord, Bob." He stands up, raises his hands, and starts to say, "I believe in God the Father almighty, Maker of ..."

You can imagine the perplexed silence of the audience. You can also imagine the host (who can sense people all over the country reaching for their remotes) jumping in and saying, "Well, that's fabulous, John, it's just really great. Praise God. But look, tell us what God did for you."

I wouldn't blame him (much). Most of us, including me, would respond with perplexed silence and a desire to find out what's on the other channels. Praising God in the words of a creed is not the sort of thing we often do.

You cannot imagine a great man like Billy Graham or Cardinal Joseph Ratzinger beginning his autobiography saying, "Let me tell you what God has done in my life," and then in the very next paragraph declaring (without warning, and as if it were the most natural thing in the world), "I believe in God the Father almighty ..." They would no doubt both give their lives for any one of the truths declared in the Nicene Creed, but they probably would not think of including it in their life's story. None of us would.

The Great Story

In St. Patrick's *Confession* we have a hint of what the early Christians thought about getting the words right. They wanted to get the words exactly right because they wanted to tell a great story. They saw the Christian teaching as the great story of the cosmos, as the story into which their own small stories fit and in which they found their meaning.

When Patrick looked at his own life, he saw it first in terms of what God has done for the universe. The story of some poor kid who gets captured by invaders, dragged off to another country, and sold into slavery, who spends years watching someone's sheep before escaping, doesn't interest him *except* as it relates to the God whose Son became Man and in dying defeated death.

You find this sort of thing all through the works of early Christians. No matter what subject they addressed, they seemed unable to write about it without telling the reader what they thought about God. After awhile, one feels that had an early Christian written a cookbook, he would have recited a creed before sharing the first recipe. And not unreasonably, if you think about it, for the reason that we have food to cook is that God is "maker of heaven and earth."

You see now, I hope, what knowing the real Jesus meant to the first few generations of Christians. They loved him, and they knew him, and so they couldn't help but talk about him in the most accurate and complete words they knew.

The real Jesus had a detailed life story. Every detail mattered if you wanted to know the real Jesus. The saints who loved him insisted that we get the words exactly right, as a photographer taking pictures of someone he loves wants everything perfect—the camera, the lighting, the background, the film, the focus—so that everyone else who sees the picture will begin to love him too.

FOUR

HATING THE WRONG WORDS

Every detail matters, if you want to know the real Jesus. This we understand easily enough. But if every detail matters, those who get the details wrong are a great problem. They challenge Jesus' friends, because they change the picture of Jesus.

Worse, they endanger men and women who want to meet Jesus but don't know him well enough to tell the real Jesus from the frauds and counterfeits. The version they promote is usually close enough to fool some Christians and a lot of would-be Christians.

The early Christians who fought for the right words were conservationists taking care of their spiritual country's greatest treasures. They only fought because someone else was trying to steal the treasures and replace them with fakes. They only started shooting when the thieves opened fire.

The Apostolic Style

For this reason we see this love of getting the words exactly right also in the early Christians' treatment of those who used the wrong words about Jesus and refused to give them up. They did not treat people in error the way we do.

They did not seem to believe in "dialogue." They were not open to questions when the answers had already been given. They did not think a claim to teach something new was simply a disagreement among friends or an argument within the family. The early Christians would have broken up many a modern church meeting.

Take St. Polycarp, for example. He had been taught by apostles and had talked with many who had seen Christ. As a bishop, St. Irenaeus reported, he had "always taught the things which he had learned from the apostles, and which the Church has handed down, and which alone are true."

We can assume that when he acted and spoke as I will describe, he was acting in the apostolic style or mode, especially considering that all the other early Christians acted and spoke in the same way. As they treated those in error, so St. Paul or St. John would have treated the same people. If this is true (and it is), the early Christians were doing what Jesus wanted them to do. The "religion of Jesus" in which everyone is pals with everyone else is not in fact the religion Jesus taught.

You are squirming again. I should warn you that much of what you will read in this chapter may offend you. Almost no one today speaks of (and to) those in error the way the early Christians did, other than a few cranks who seem to take too much pleasure in attack, and who sin against charity in responding to those who sin against truth.

When we happen to read the word "heretic" or "apostate" in the letters section of a religious magazine, most of us immediately think of the writer flailing away at the keys with the veins bulging in his forehead, a decidedly crazy look in his eyes, beside him a stack of the kind of newspaper printed in very tiny type, except for the headlines. I've known such people, and I avoid them.

I do not want to upset you, but please ask yourself if such a fellow might be right in principle if not in practice. We know he's a bad example, but that doesn't answer for us the question of what to do with people who get the words wrong on purpose. We still have to decide how to respond to people who sell pictures of Jesus that don't look like him.

We have a choice to make, as we always do when we read the early Christians. We can assume they were, in general, right in the way they treated those in error, or we can assume that they were, in general, wrong.

If you have agreed with me so far in submitting to the saints, you should not stop now. You should assume that they were right, and that there must be a modern way to do with error—willful error, remember—what they did with it. We must love the people who get the words wrong as the Lord loves them, of course. The question for us is how to love them while saying what we must say to them and to others about their refusal to know the real Jesus and their lying about him in public.

Enemies of Faith

Let me start by telling some of the stories that make modern people squirm. According to St. Polycarp, the apostle John went to the public bath in Ephesus and found a Gnostic teacher named Cerinthus inside. John ran out before he took his bath, crying, "Let us fly, lest even the bathhouse fall down, because Cerinthus, the enemy of the truth, is within." Polycarp approved of this.

St. Irenaeus, who had grown up listening to Polycarp, said that when Polycarp heard an error, he would "stop his ears, as was his custom, and exclaim, 'O good God, unto what times have you spared me that I should endure these things?' And he would flee the place where, sitting or standing, he had heard such words."

Polycarp himself once met Marcion, apparently on a street in Rome. Marcion asked him, with what seems in retrospect very little sense, "Do you know me?" Polycarp answered, "I do know you. You're the firstborn of Satan." One suspects the conversation deteriorated from there.

On second thought, I am not so sure that Marcion acted with little sense. Judging from the examples of such men through history, those who insisted on saying the wrong words about Jesus were often oddly boastful and aggressive, even smug.

When you and I would have retired quietly to some out-of-the-way village where we could hold our ideas in peace, they put themselves forward, often at the risk of their lives. They did this, the early Christians would have said, because their errors grew from a selfish desire to assert themselves against the Church, and ego always insists on being recognized.

According to Irenaeus, the reason there were so many false ideas around was that people are vain and greedy. They all want to be teachers—we might say gurus—and so they leave their teacher and come up with a new one they can call their own, which they present as a new and improved version of the now outdated Christianity.

Marcion may have come up to Polycarp in the hope of being recognized as a fellow Christian teacher, or he may have swaggered up to him hoping to be denounced, thereby proving that he was specially enlightened and the Christians not. In either case, Polycarp wouldn't speak to him after pronouncing judgment.

Such, Irenaeus wrote, "was the horror which the apostles and their disciples had against holding even verbal communication with any corrupters of the truth. As Paul also says, 'A man that is an heretic, after the first and second admonition, reject; knowing that he that is such is subverted, and sins, being condemned of himself'" (Ti 3:10).

Marcion's Errors

As you might have guessed, Marcion got a lot of this kind of response. St. Justin Martyr, who lived at the same time as Marcion, accused him of serving the devil, because he said that God didn't make the universe.

This the early Christians often said about those in error. As St. Vincent of Lerins said two centuries later: "We may be assured beyond doubt, when we find people alleging passages from the apostles or prophets against the Catholic faith, that the devil speaks through their mouths." (Vincent, you may remember, was the one who defined the Catholic faith as "that faith which has been believed everywhere, always, and by all.")

St. Irenaeus described Marcion as one who was "speaking as with the mouth of the devil" and referred to "the serpent which was in Marcion." He spoke of Marcion and his peers as "malignant-minded people," examples of "an abyss of madness and of blasphemy against Christ." In the second and third books of

Against Heresies, he took apart Marcion's arguments with a restrained but effective sarcasm.

In the fifth and last book, he summed up his case against Marcion, and he did not pull his punches. Marcion is one of those "who blaspheme the Creator." He and his peers are to "be recognized as agents of Satan by all those who worship God; through whose agency Satan now, and not before, has been seen to speak against God, even him who has prepared eternal fire for every kind of apostasy."

What he then argued is quite interesting. He argued from Marcion's teaching to his motives. He found in Marcion's rejection of the creator God the rationalization of his own depravity. When criminals are caught, he wrote, they blame those who make the laws, not themselves. In the same way men like Marcion, who are "filled with a satanic spirit,"

> bring innumerable accusations against our Creator, who has both given to us the spirit of life, and established a law adapted for all; and they will not admit that the judgment of God is just. Wherefore also they set about imagining some other Father who neither cares about nor exercises a providence over our affairs, nay, one who even approves of all sins.

They wanted, he argued, a God who would let them do what they want. The creator God of the Scriptures gave rules they didn't like, and therefore they treated him as a bad god and invented one too far away to tell them what to do.

Whether or not he was right about Marcion—and there's no reason to doubt he was—Irenaeus understood fallen men and women. Sinful people don't like the truth and therefore they rewrite it, and from the way they rewrite it we can often tell what parts of it they most disliked.

Abusive Tertullian

The early third-century writer Tertullian (he died about 225) wrote of Marcion in a typically brutal way. (Tertullian may have been a lawyer.) I am not recommending him as an example. He was not a saint—later in his life he joined an odd sect called the Montanists—and therefore not one of our guides, but his way of speaking does show how deeply the early Christians hated the wrong words Marcion said about Jesus.

His treatise *Against Marcion* begins with stunning abuse. After describing how horrible is the country of Pontus from which Marcion came, he declared that nothing in the country

is so barbarous and sad as the fact that Marcion was born there, fouler than any Scythian, more roving than the wagon-life of the Sarmatian, more inhuman than the Massagete, more audacious than an Amazon, darker than the cloud [of Pontus], colder than its winter, more brittle than its ice, more deceitful than the Ister, more craggy than Caucasus.

Even "the true Prometheus, Almighty God, is mangled by Marcion's blasphemies," Tertullian went on. He was just warming up. "Marcion is more savage than even the beasts of that barbarous region. For what beaver was ever a greater emasculator than he who has abolished the nuptial bond? What Pontic mouse ever had such gnawing powers as he who has gnawed the Gospels to pieces?" (And you thought beavers were cute.)

Of all the early Christians, Tertullian may be the very worst model for us, because he seems to have enjoyed writing such abuse. He was the third-century Church's pit bull. But you must remember that the provocation to write in such a way was great.

The picture of Jesus that Marcion had drawn looked enough like the real Jesus to fool people, but it wasn't really a picture of Jesus at all. Marcion was leading people away from God into what St. Irenaeus had called "an abyss of madness and of blasphemy."

Think of what staid newspapers like *The New York Times* have said about companies that poisoned the water in a neighborhood and then let people live there without warning them. Tertullian, and all the other early Christians, knew that spiritual poison was much deadlier, and that is why they spoke as they did.

Is This Christlike?

Here you may be squirming in your chair again. (I did warn you.) Is this, well, Christlike? you ask. Even leaving out Tertullian, all the others weren't much kinder to their enemies. And they were *saints*.

Presumably (you continue) Cerinthus and Marcion meant well. And even if they didn't, you don't convert someone by calling him the enemy of truth or the firstborn of Satan in public. What about the soft answer that turns away wrath that Proverbs 15:1 tells us to give? Didn't St. Paul say in Romans 12:18 to live peaceably with all men if you could?

And further, Christians shouldn't fight about small differences in wording. In a world where almost no one knows the Lord, they shouldn't have fought among themselves over who he is. Especially with the Romans' going on occasional persecuting binges, the early Christians should not have alienated their comrades and friends. We're all in this together. Just why are you offering these people as an example to us? Would you let your children speak to someone in that way?

Well, I might, you know. If someday someone denies our Lord while pretending to represent him, and my children are the only ones able to respond, I hope they will say, "That's a heresy. That's not who Jesus is." I hope they will be more polite than Tertullian, but I couldn't object to their calling the wrong words the wrong words, even if they upset the speaker.

But you do have a point. A Christian isn't allowed to be rude to people like Marcion just because they're making a big mistake. Even so, this doesn't let you off the hook, because the early Christians weren't being rude. Given the provocation, they were being scrupulously polite.

How We Differ

Here's another matter on which we modern Christians differ so radically from our brothers and sisters of the first few centuries: They would have pointed out that St. Paul had said to live peaceably with all men *and* to avoid the company of former Christians who wouldn't repent of their errors.

In cases like this, we almost always take one of Paul's instructions but not the other. We're the kid on the seesaw sitting on the ground but still proud of his balance. It's easier to sit that way, after all. Balancing is hard.

For that matter, the early Christians had a better idea of what is Christlike than we do. Jesus himself often spoke rather sharply to people who refused him. Take one famous example. Jesus called the scribes and Pharisees "whitewashed tombs" and a "brood of vipers" (Mt 23:27, 29). In our terms, he was calling them "rotting meat" and "poisonous little vermin."

If he spoke to them today, he might compare the scribes and Pharisees to one of those old stone sewage treatment plants, built in a neo-Gothic style to look like a church or a castle. He would tell them, in public, "You may look like Chartres cathedral on the outside, but on the inside you're full of excrement." *We* cringe at his language. You can guess how the scribes and Pharisees felt.

You can find in the Gospels several other examples of Jesus' speaking to hostile listeners in the same way. He was not speaking this way to insult them but to change them if they would really listen. If they were insulted, as they usually seem to have been (and I would have been too), that only proves that they didn't know who was speaking to them. Whatever God says to you, it is, by definition, not insulting.

The scribes and Pharisees were men he would die for in just a few months. But he would also tell them the truth about themselves, in language they could not ignore, and force them to a decision to repent and follow him, or not.

The Mind of Christ

This is not an excuse for us to insult the people who call Jesus by the wrong words, even if the names we call them are perfectly accurate. You and I are not the Lord, nor yet saints. We are only his disciples and their pupils, and some of the things they did should come with the label "Kids, don't try this at home."

I do not want to encourage people to abuse each other. But I do not want to encourage misleading silence either. You will want to be truly Christlike, which will sometimes force you to speak like Jesus or St. Polycarp or St. Irenaeus, though perhaps not quite like Tertullian.

To speak rightly, we need to grow in the mind of Christ. The saints we are following had enough of the mind of Christ to know when to speak in such terms. When they called a man like Marcion "the firstborn of Satan," they were being kind. (Stop snorting. I'm serious about this.) To identify his master was an act of charity to him, offered that he might see himself as he really was and repent. This was the only chance he had to escape his master and his master's end in hell.

When the saints called a man "the firstborn of Satan," they were also being kind to those he might fool. They needed to sound the alarm, and it needed to sound like an alarm. A few years ago someone invented an alarm clock that played ocean sounds instead of buzzing, and whoever bought the clock was late to work the next day.

The early Christians could not take the chance that their alarm would not wake up people who needed to wake up. It would not do to say, "Our brother Marcion has raised some very serious questions for us, and we are deeply grateful to him for doing so, and we want to thank him for modeling a way of engaging these very complex problems that we are all struggling with, and for giving us some very creative answers, but after due consideration we feel that some of his answers are not fully in accord with the Church's teaching, but we hope he will continue this very enriching dialogue."

By telling the truth about Marcion and telling people whose servant he was, St. Polycarp, St. Irenaeus, and the others showed their love for those tempted to follow him. Like any competent teacher, Marcion knew how to make his teaching attractive and even compelling. Unless they spoke as they did, some people would follow Marcion's Jesus and therefore never meet the real one, the one who for us men and our salvation became man.

Peaceable Living

St. Paul did say to live peaceably with all men if you could. He also said rather often in his letters that you cannot live peaceably with people who get the words wrong and try to teach the wrong words to others (Gal 1:8-9, for example). "Peace" does not mean surrender, and it does not mean silence. If it had, Paul would have died at home in his bed.

The early Christians were deeply Pauline. And Johannine, and Petrine, and Jamesian too. In this book we see the saints of the early centuries doing their duty to defend the faith, to make sure that all Christians got the words exactly right. In fighting over words they knew themselves to be fighting for human souls. They were forced to confront people who got the words wrong, who often knew exactly what they were doing and were very good at it.

This explains the way they wrote about those who insisted on teaching the wrong words. Yet we should not think that attacking error was the thing they liked most to do. With the exception of Tertullian and a few others, the early Christians did not like to fight, and one suspects when reading them that they really didn't want to write books such as *Against Heresies,* but knew they had to.

The saints to whose guidance we're looking loved the Lord Jesus and loved to tell others about him. That is what they wanted to do. Fighting those who told others the wrong things about him is what they were forced to do.

I did just say that the saints' example was a dangerous one to follow for those of us in whom the mind of Christ is not nearly as well formed. As a writer, I can tell you how exciting is rhetorical blood lust. Getting the bad guy in your sights and pulling the trigger is a lot of fun, and addicting fun too.

But nevertheless, the saints' example is also a dangerous one not to follow. Just as many people are drawing bad pictures of Jesus now as then, and just as many people are following them. If you've been blessed to see the real picture, you may be the one called to denounce the bad ones.

An Early Example

When we turn from the judgments of the bishops to the judgments of their people, we find the same energetic insistence on getting the words exactly right and refusing anyone who got them wrong. In fact, in the middle of the third century most of the bishops accepted the wrong words, and it was the laity who refused to speak to them until the bishops came back to the truth.

The error they opposed was Arianism. Arianism, you may remember from the second chapter, argued that Jesus was the Son of God but not completely God. The difference seemed to depend on a technical and obscure philosophical disagreement about when Jesus was begotten of the Father. We might be surprised that the laity of the day could even tell the difference.

The Arians wanted to make sure that Christians didn't make God less than God, so they said that his Son was in some sense his creation. They could still speak of Jesus in almost the same way as everyone else and preach him as the world's Savior. But at the Council of Nicaea in 325, the Church's bishops had decided that—whatever the Arians thought they were doing—their teaching denied the Lord and could not be tolerated.

The error persisted, evolving into new forms. Though the Arians had been so soundly defeated at Nicaea, by the middle of the century they dominated much of the eastern Church and more often than not had the support of the emperor. With his support they could exile the bishops and priests loyal to Nicaea and replace them with Arians.

Samosatan Resistance

The bishops kept giving in, but the people fought. Not all of them, alas, but a surprising number—the "better laity," as St.

Basil of Caesarea called them. We can take the example of the people of Samosata, a city on the upper Euphrates River, who resisted the Arians with admirable single-mindedness.

In 374 the Arians exiled the Samosatans' bishop, St. Eusebius—who later died when an Arian woman hit him in the head with a brick—and appointed a man named Eunomius to replace him. (This Eusebius is not the famous "father of Church history," Eusebius of Caesarea, who died in 340. There were five famous Eusebiuses in the fourth century.)

Writing a few decades later, the historian Theodoret reported that in Samosata "not an inhabitant of the city, were he herding in indigence or blazing in wealth, not a servant, not a handi-craftsman, not a farm worker, not a gardener, nor man nor woman, whether young or old, came to gatherings in church. The new bishop lived all alone; not a soul looked at him, or exchanged a word with him."

The new bishop seems to have been a nice man, at least he "behaved with courteous moderation," according to Theodoret. One day at the public baths, noticing that his servants had shut the doors to keep out everyone else, he ordered them to open the doors and let the people in.

Having done that, he saw that the people were still standing outside the bath and thought they did so as a sign of respect to him as their bishop. Instead, they believed "that even the water was affected with the pollution of his heresy," and were not going to touch water that had touched him. When he found this out, Eunomius left the bath. The people then ordered the baths to be drained and filled with fresh water before they would bathe. Eunomius left town.

But the Arians weren't done. They appointed another

bishop, Lucius, "an unmistakable wolf, and enemy of the sheep." The people of Samosata were not done, either. Faced with a more vicious wolf than the moderate Eunomius, "the sheep, all shepherdless as they were, shepherded themselves, and persistently preserved the apostolic doctrine in all its purity."

Theodoret told the story of some boys playing in the street, whose ball rolled between the feet of the donkey on which Lucius was riding. The boys started yelling because they thought that their ball was polluted by coming so close to an Arian, and after lighting a fire threw the ball through the flames to purify it.

"I know indeed that this was but a boyish act, and a survival of the ancient ways," Theodoret admitted, "but it is nonetheless sufficient to prove in what hatred the town held the Arian faction." This angered Lucius, as you can guess, but the people did not back down.

When the Arians finally lost power, the people did not "let bygones be bygones" and act as if nothing had really happened. Some years later Eusebius' nephew Antiochus was elected bishop of Samosata. He had been sent into exile by Lucius.

When he knelt before the altar to be consecrated, he turned and saw that a bishop who had "for some little time had held a communion with the Arians" had placed a hand upon him. "Plucking the hand away he bade him be gone from among the consecrators, saying that he could not endure a right hand which had received mysteries [the Eucharist] blasphemously celebrated."

Other Examples

I could give other examples of the laity's refusal to submit to Arian bishops, even when most of the bishops had joined the Arian party and in various councils seemed to settle the question of what Christians believed. The resistance to these Arians cost the people a lot.

Writing to the bishops of Italy and France about 372, St. Basil told of the "better laity" in Cappadocia staying away from the Arian churches, which he called "schools of impiety." They walked out of the cities where they would "lift their hands in the deserts with sighs and tears to their Lord in heaven."

In "the thirteenth year since the war of heresy began against us," he wrote friends in the West about four years later,

The sum and substance of our troubles is this: The people have left the houses of prayer and are holding congregations in the wildernesses. It is a sad sight. Women, boys, old men, and those who are in other ways infirm, remain in the open air, in heavy rain, in the snow, the gales and the frost of winter as well as in summer under the blazing heat of the sun. All this they are suffering because they refuse to have anything to do with the wicked leaven of Arius.

About the same time, St. Hilary of Poitiers in France wrote to the Emperor Constantius, asking him to help the churches who were being suppressed by the Arians with the emperor's approval. "They who fear the Lord God and his judgment should not be polluted and contaminated with execrable blasphemies…. It is impossible, it is unreasonable, to mix true and false, to confuse light and darkness, and bring into union, of whatever kind, night and day."

The letter was a bold one. He must have known it would infuriate the emperor, given what he said about the emperor's religious allies, and it got him sent into exile in Asia. In God's providence, however, this worked to his good, for Hilary, though a Western bishop, knew the Greek language and Eastern theology, and now he was actually living in the East. It also made him a hero in the West, as one of the first Western bishops to suffer for the faith.

Hilary's Defense

St. Hilary was one of those who wanted very much to get the words right, and suffered for it. He was also one of those who understood what getting the words right required and would not compromise when compromise left any chance that other people might get the words wrong.

Here is yet another way the early Christians differed from us: They not only condemned error with a certainty and thoroughness that makes us uncomfortable, they made sure that those in error couldn't pretend to hold the faith of the Church. They did not believe in a tactful ambiguity or breadth. They would not buy peace in the community of the Church at the cost of clarity in the teaching.

Take, for example, Hilary's response to a creed produced by an Arian council held in the city of Sirmium in 357. He called it "the Blasphemy of Sirmium," and the name stuck. This "godless confession," "pestilent and godless blasphemy," "impious and infidel creed," as he called it, forbade any use of the word "essence" (*ousia*) because it bothered some Christians, Scripture never used the word, and no one could know the truth of the matter anyway.

It spoke reverently of God the Father, insisted on the "Catholic doctrine" that the Son had "been begotten from the Father" and was "God of God, light of light," and declared that "the Son of God himself, our Lord and God ... took flesh or body, that is man, from the womb of the Virgin Mary." It declared that "the Trinity must always be preserved."

So far, so good. But it also said that the Father is "greater than the Son in honor, dignity, splendor, majesty, and in the very name of Father, the Son himself testifying 'He who sent me is greater than I.'"

This was the problem, and Hilary knew it was a fatal problem. (Remember the experiment in the second chapter? If one Sunday you replaced the Nicene Creed with the Blasphemy of Sirmium, I suspect that nineteen out of twenty people would say it without blinking, despite its demotion of Jesus from the Godhead.)

Banning the word "essence" seemed to be fair to the Arians and the Nicaeans. If the Church was divided by a word, and an unbiblical word at that, simply ban the word and reestablish peace. They could find a form of words that both sides could use together, even if they did not mean quite the same thing by it. They would not let a technical philosophical question about the nature of essence in the Godhead divide Christians.

For the Arians to ban any word using "essence" was much cleverer than it may appear. This supposedly fair and peace-making restriction hit the Nicaeans very hard—as the people who approved it intended it to do—for it took away the word by which the bishops at the Council of Nicaea had established the equality of the Son with the Father thirty-two years before. It was the word that had removed any possibility of an Arian reading of Scripture.

Hilary would not accept this, especially as it was coupled with an implicitly Arian view of Jesus. This creed, he declared, was blasphemy. It was not an honest mistake, or a stage in the dialogue, or a possible reading of Scripture, or an exploration of new questions, or a reasonable interpretation of the evidence. It was an offense against God himself.

"Knowing Not God"

St. Hilary was not slow to declare that those who insisted on getting the words wrong were not Christians. "He clearly knows not wisdom who knows not God," he wrote of the Arians in his *On the Trinity*.

> And since Christ is Wisdom, he who knows not Christ or hates him is beyond the pale of wisdom. As, for instance, they who will have it that the Lord of glory, and King of the universe, and only-begotten God is a creature of God and not his Son, and in addition to such foolish lies show a still more foolish cleverness in the defense of their falsehood.

For Hilary, knowing Jesus meant getting the words you say about him right. If you said, as the Arians did, that he was in some sense a creature, you didn't know him. If you spoke of him as less than the Father in honor, dignity, and the rest rather than as "of one essence" with the Father, you did not know him. And if you did not know him, you did not know God his Father, even if you thought (as the Arians did) that you were protecting the Father in the way you spoke of the Son.

The logic of this may not strike a modern reader right away. We don't think that intellectual mistakes have consequences. Miscalculating a flight path from Los Angeles to Tokyo, leaving out a "not" in an important piece of legislation, adding an extra zero to your income tax deduction: We know these mistakes cause problems. But to delete "of one essence" from the philosophical section of a Christian teaching, this we don't feel to be a problem.

If the saints were right, however, it is a big problem. What Hilary was saying, and what almost any of the early saints would have said with him, is that the man who says he loves the Lord Jesus Christ but still insists that Christ is inferior to the Father, is not a Christian.

The Arian picture of Jesus is not a picture of the real Jesus. The differences may be hard to see, but the one who knows and loves the real Jesus will see them and reject the picture as a forgery or a counterfeit. The one who loves the real Jesus will not want a picture that looks "pretty much like him."

It is the difference between a perfect picture and one in which the subject's brown eyes have been turned blue. The person who does not know him well will say that it looks a bit funny, but it's him all right. The person who knows him well will say that it looks a lot like him, but it isn't him at all.

By refusing the word "of one essence," the Arian was in great danger of being among those who say, "Lord, Lord," but to whom the Lord says, "I never knew you. Depart from me" (Mt 7:23). He would not know them because they had refused to know him.

No Honest Mistakes

The early Christians did not seem to have a place for what we would call "honest mistakes" or "differences of opinion" in teaching about Christ. Remember what St. Leo said of Eutyches, and what St. Polycarp, St. Irenaeus, and St. Justin Martyr said about Marcion.

They believed that those in error were really in danger because they were cutting themselves off from the Church and from God. They wouldn't try to jolly them along, or invite them to stay till they saw the light, if they ever did. They told them they were making a mistake, and they often told them just who it was that mistake served.

But that isn't all they did. They would try to bring those who got it wrong to repentance, not only through warning but through kindness, mostly the kindness of praying for them.

You will probably ask, remembering the fellow flailing at the keyboard, how we can speak this way without turning into brutes and bullies. To this question too the early Christians give us an answer. They give it to us mostly by example. The answer is: We need to show implacable and unending resistance to error, offered from a heart convinced of its own unworthiness, with the hope that those in error may repent.

"Let us likewise deal kindly, let us persuade our adversaries of that which is to their profit," said St. Ambrose of Milan in 378, writing against the Arians. "For we would not overthrow, but rather heal. We lay no ambush for them, but warn them as in duty bound. Kindliness often bends those whom neither force nor argument will avail to overcome." (He did, however, a few paragraphs later say that "if our adversaries cannot be turned by kindness, let us summon them before the Judge," meaning the Lord. He knew the Lord would convict them.)

Even when telling the people of Smyrna not even to meet with false teachers, whom he called "beasts in the shape of men," St. Ignatius also told them "you must pray to God for them, if by any means they may be brought to repentance, which, however, will be very difficult. Yet Jesus Christ, who is our true life, has the power of [effecting] this."

A Caution

I have said that the saints to whom we are looking for guidance knew how to speak the hard word because they thought with the mind of Christ. Let me add that although they knew how important it was to get the words exactly right, they also knew that the Church and its witness suffered whenever Christians fought.

In one of the letters already quoted, St. Basil said that "now the very vindication of orthodoxy is looked upon in some quarters as an opportunity for mutual attack, and men conceal their private ill-will and pretend that their hostility is all for the sake of the truth." The need to say the right words will tempt many of us to feel good about ourselves for saying hard and cruel words. "The saddest thing about it all," he continued,

> is that the sound part is divided against itself, and the troubles we are suffering are like those which once befell Jerusalem when Vespasian was besieging it. The Jews of that time were at once beset by foes without and consumed by the internal sedition of their own people. In our case, too, in addition to the open attack of the heretics, the churches are reduced to utter helplessness by the war raging among those who are supposed to be orthodox.

Arguments, even arguments you have to join, weakened the appeal of the faith to those outside the Church and weakened the confidence of those inside. "All the while unbelievers laugh, men of weak faith are shaken; faith is uncertain," Basil said. When Christians fought, the people who didn't believe would not come closer; the Christians who had trouble believing were tempted to stop; and even those who did firmly believe felt as if the foundation might fail.

But all this said, Basil insisted that the cause of the problem was not the fact that Christians disagreed and insisted on their own teaching rather than living in peace. The problem was that some who claimed to be Christians taught lies. "Souls are drenched in ignorance," he said, "because adulterators of the word imitate the truth." Though they understood the cost of conflict, the early Christians had no choice but to fight the adulterators of the word.

Fighting over words is a dangerous thing to do when they are words about God. But the early Christians fought nevertheless, because when people get the words wrong, unbelievers are given an excuse to scoff at Christ and not face him, men and women who hold to the faith but not with confidence begin to lose their hold, and people for whom Christ died simply do not know who he is.

In the Midst of Wolves

In this chapter we have looked at the way in which the early Christian saints confronted those who taught a fake Jesus, in which they imitated the way our Lord confronted the scribes and Pharisees. This was only one part of his life that they tried to imitate, and not the main part.

The saints also imitated Jesus' death on the cross. The man who called the scribes and Pharisees "white-washed tombs" was also the man who took their sins upon himself and took those sins to the grave. The saints managed this combination a lot better than we do. We'd be wrong to read their words as if they were like us, and assume that when they called a man "the firstborn of Satan" they did it with pleasure or a feeling of self-satisfaction.

Even in the fiercest argument, the early Christian saints seem to have remembered that Jesus' strength "is made perfect in weakness" (2 Cor 12:18). I don't mean this in a sentimental way. The weakness I mean was not a weakness of conviction, or timidity, or a fear of speaking up. It was the weakness of sheep who nevertheless conquer wolves. (You may be thinking that if these early Christians were sheep, they were sheep that bit.)

The early Christians tried to be "as harmless as doves and wise as serpents," and to live "as sheep among wolves" (Mt 10:16).

As St. John Chrysostom explained in his sermon on this verse, Jesus shows his strength when "sheep get the better of wolves" because the wolves have bitten them one thousand times but not changed their spirit or their minds. This, he said, was a greater miracle than their not being eaten.

Christians should be ashamed "who set like wolves upon our enemies," he continued. "For so long as we are sheep, we conquer: though ten thousand wolves prowl around, we overcome and prevail. But if we become wolves, we are worsted, for the help of our Shepherd departs from us. For he feeds not wolves, but sheep."

What did Jesus mean by being "wise as a serpent"? John continued. The serpent, he said, will give up its body to save its head. In the same way, Jesus wants us to "give up everything but the faith, though goods, body, life itself must be yielded. For that [the faith] is the head and the root; and if that be preserved, though you lose all, you will recover all with so much the more splendor."

Triumphant Sheep

The idea that responding to the wolves like sheep will lead to triumph does not, St. John admitted, seem probable. To tell a sheep that he'll flourish among a pack of hungry wolves is to speak "as though one should cast a reed into fire, and command it not to be burnt by the fire, but to quench it." But this has actually happened among people just like us, he reminded his hearers.

Jesus, who told us to be sheep among wolves, "knows the nature of things. He knows that fierceness is not quenched by fierceness, but by gentleness." We see this reality proved in the book of Acts, in the lives of Jesus' close friends, he insisted. Whenever the apostles' enemies rose against them, they imitated the dove and answered meekly, and by doing so "did away with their wrath, quenched their madness, broke their impetuosity.... Do you see how we must be perfect on all points, so as neither to be abased by dangers, nor provoked by anger?"

To be perfect in all ways, and neither scared of the world nor speaking against it in anger, is a good summary of the mind of the early Christian saints on the need to get the words exactly right. They wanted to be harmless as doves and wise as serpents, and they managed that balance to an extent we find hard to believe. We find it hard to believe, I suspect, because we ourselves couldn't manage it.

They were willing to fight when they had to, but they wanted peace. "One should adjust one's degrees of flexibility and rigidity so as not to give way to all and sundry simply through cowardice, nor to cut oneself off from others by being foolhardy," wrote St. Gregory of Nazianzus. As members of the same body, "it is better and of more use to adapt ourselves to one another, than to begin by condemning one another, then breaking off from one another, then destroying our confidence in one another by living in separation."

But though they wanted peace, it had to be the peace of unity in the truth. "Let no one be under the impression that I am saying that we must always look for peace," Gregory continued. "... Just as it is sometimes better to have disagreement, so on occasions, agreement can be worse than discord."

We misread the early Christians if we think they cared so much for getting the words right because they needed to have everything their own way. It is hard for us, trained as we have been to think that every conflict is a fight over power and control, to realize that some men may have fought for truth and love.

They loved the real Jesus. They knew who he was. They wanted other people to know and love him too. But some effective preachers were lying about Jesus and getting vulnerable people to follow a Jesus who didn't exist and couldn't save them. To agree with these people was worse, much worse, than discord.

His Wounds

I am reminded of a story about the fourth-century bishop of Tours in France, St. Martin. One day as Martin was praying in his cell, a young man appeared in a purple light, wearing a gold crown and gold shoes. He said to Martin, "Acknowledge, Martin, who it is that you behold. I am Christ; and being just about to descend to earth, I wished first to manifest myself to you." Martin didn't say anything, so the young man asked him, "Martin, why do you hesitate to believe, when you see? I am Christ."

Then Martin said: "The Lord Jesus did not predict that he would come clothed in purple, and with a glittering crown upon his head. I will not believe that Christ has come, unless he appears with that appearance and form in which he suffered, and openly displaying the marks of his wounds upon the cross." The young man vanished, leaving a disgusting smell in the room, proving that he had really been the devil.

Would you have said what Martin said? I'm not sure I would have. Would you have worshiped the young man in purple? I think I might have. He obviously looked like someone who ought to be worshiped.

Even the devil can make himself look like the real Jesus to trick people who don't know exactly who Jesus is and exactly what he looks like. This is why the early Christian saints, who were truly obedient sheep who followed the Shepherd in every way they could, charged into battle and bit his enemies.

FIVE

THE WORD AND THE RIGHT WORDS

At this point you may be asking, "Doesn't Scripture tell us clearly enough who Jesus really is? Why should anyone care to get the words exactly right when we can all just open our Bibles and find the answer?"

This way of thinking presumes that if we read Scripture and still can't find the answer to a question, God must not care whether we know it. It must not matter to him that we get all the words exactly right. You can obviously know the real Jesus without knowing everything about him—what he did from the age of twelve to thirty, for example—just as a man can know his wife without knowing her blood type or the prescription to her glasses or her fourth-grade report card.

"Isn't Scripture clear enough that we don't need to get the words exactly right?" is one of those great questions to which the answer is: well, yes and no.

The Saints' Yes

The early Christian saints would say yes, period. But I say "yes and no" because what they meant by "yes" is not quite what we mean by "yes." I will explain this in a minute.

"The entire Scriptures, the Prophets, and the Gospels, can be clearly, unambiguously, and harmoniously understood by all," said St. Irenaeus in the late second century. "The canon of Scripture is complete, and sufficient of itself for everything, and more than sufficient," said St. Vincent of Lerins about 250 years later. Everyone in between would have said exactly the same thing.

Except some of the heretics, that is, which was one of the ways you could spot them. The Christianized Gnostics claimed to have a special insight into the real meaning of Scripture, and they also claimed to carry a secret tradition of crucial truths not found in it. Marcion declared that most of the Scriptures couldn't be trusted, and even the parts he trusted had to be edited first.

Against this sort of thing, the early Christians insisted that Scripture is both clear and comprehensive. If Irenaeus and Vincent and the rest spoke to a meeting of Christians today, they might well find themselves denounced as "fundamentalists"— which would surprise them, because they were only saying what Christians said.

In his lectures to people preparing for baptism, St. Cyril of Jerusalem warned his hearers not to believe anything he said, not even an off-the-cuff remark, unless it could be proven from the Scriptures.

For concerning the divine and holy mysteries of the faith, not even a casual statement must be delivered without the Holy Scriptures; nor must we be drawn aside by mere plausibility and artifices of speech. Even to me, who tell you these things, do not give absolute credence, unless you receive the proof of the things which I announce from the divine Scriptures. For this salvation which we believe depends not on ingenious reasoning, but on demonstration from the Holy Scriptures.

"The sacred and inspired Scriptures are sufficient to declare the truth," said St. Athanasius. Even when defending the decision of the bishops at Nicaea to use the term "of one essence," which was not to be found in Scripture, he noted that "the tokens of truth are more exact as drawn from Scripture, than from other sources."

In defending his teaching against his critics, St. Basil of Caesarea said, "Let God-inspired Scripture decide between us. On whichever side be found doctrines in harmony with the word of God, in favor of that side will be cast the vote of truth."

"For among the things that are plainly laid down in Scripture are to be found all matters that concern faith and the manner of life," said St. Augustine.

St. John Chrysostom declared that "all things are dear and open that are in the divine Scriptures; the necessary things are all plain." In the Scriptures, he told his people, "you have the oracles of God." Not knowing the Scriptures is "the cause of all evils," and a cause of weakness as well, for without them, "We go into battle without arms, and how can we come off safe?"

This explains John's astonishment that the Christians of his day took the Scriptures so lightly. (Some things don't change.) When they come to church, he lamented, "They do not lay to heart, they do not consider, that they are entering into the presence of God, that it is he who addresses them." They do not listen with reverence even when the reader declares, "Thus says the Lord," and the deacon demands silence for the reading.

They would pay attention if they realized God was speaking through the writers, he said. "For if when rulers are addressing them, they do not allow their minds to wander, much less would they, when God is speaking. We are ministers, beloved. We speak not our own things, but the things of God. Letters coming from heaven are every day read."

Their view of Scripture explains the early Christian's way of writing. They left us long passages that are almost simply strings of verses, put into the order they needed for their argument. Rarely did they explain or argue anything without quoting Scripture. They quoted Scripture so much that several modern writers have observed that if we had lost the Scriptures, we could nearly reassemble them from the writings of the early Christians.

The Source

The early Christians said all this so forcefully because they believed they had gotten the apostolic writings we call the New Testament from Jesus himself, through his first disciples.

Irenaeus was the first to call them the New Testament, but St. Peter had already set the pattern by treating St. Paul's letters as equal to the Hebrew Scriptures (2 Pt 3:15-16). The earliest Christian writings we have, writings that appeared just after the time of the apostles—St. Ignatius' *Letter to the Smyrnaeans, 2 Clement,* St. Justin Martyr's *Dialogue with Trypho,* and the *Epistle of Barnabas*—treat apostolic writings as Scripture.

"We have as the source of teaching," wrote St. Clement of Alexandria, "the Lord, both by the Prophets, the Gospel, and the blessed apostles, 'in divers manners and at sundry times,' leading from the beginning of knowledge to the end."

"We have learned from none others the plan of our salvation, than from those through whom the Gospel has come down to us," St. Irenaeus said. They first preached the message in public and then, "by the will of God, handed [the message] down to us in the Scriptures, to be the ground and pillar of our faith." The apostles had "perfect knowledge," for the Holy Spirit had filled them.

As we have seen before, the early Christians were certain that the earlier Christians had passed on the apostles' message. "What our Fathers have delivered, this is truly doctrine," said St. Athanasius,

> and this is truly the token of doctors, to confess the same thing with each other, and to vary neither from themselves nor from their Fathers.... For though they lived in different times, yet they one and all tend the same way, being prophets of the one God, and preaching the same Word harmoniously.

The Reader

That said, the early Christians did not believe that the Scriptures revealed the truth to everyone. When St. Irenaeus said the Scriptures could be understood by all, he did not mean anyone who happened to pick up the book. Even the Christian reader needed "a sound mind ... devoted to piety and the love of truth, [that] will eagerly meditate upon those things God has placed within the power of mankind, and has subjected to our knowledge." They must study it every day if they want to know what it says.

"Those who are ready to toil in the most excellent pursuits will not desist from the search after truth, till they get the demonstration from the Scriptures themselves," wrote St. Clement of Alexandria. They must use their wills and energy and the intellectual tools to distinguish true from false. They also had to remember that "he who hopes for everlasting rest knows also that the entrance to it is toilsome and strait."

The reader must also read the Scriptures humbly. For one thing, he must not expect to find what the Scriptures don't offer. "Seek not what is undiscoverable, for you will not discover," wrote St. Basil. "Believe what is written, seek not what is not written."

For another, the Scriptures often proclaim without explaining, and in these cases Christians must accept what the Scriptures tell them. In most of these cases they would not understand the explanations anyway.

St. John Chrysostom said, "I know that he begat the Son: the manner how, I am ignorant of. I know that the Holy Spirit is from Him; how from Him, I do not understand. I eat food, but how this is converted into my flesh and blood, I know not. We know not these things, which we see every day when we eat, yet we meddle with inquiries concerning the substance of God."

Whatever we don't understand we can still believe, because we believe in God. "It is better to believe even what is impossible to our own nature and to men, than to be unbelieving like the rest of the world," said St. Justin Martyr. "For we know that our Master Jesus Christ said that 'what is impossible with men is possible with God.'" Hell will be the reward for those "who do not believe that those things which God has taught us by Christ will come to pass."

The early Christians wrote with such certainty because they believed that the one truth of Scripture enlightened everyone, according to their needs. In his *Exhortation to Martyrdom*, St. Cyprian of Carthage wrote that he had made a compendium of the Scriptures rather than arguing the point himself, because he wanted everyone to take up the Scriptures for himself. "For if I were to give a man a garment finished and ready," he said,

> it would be my garment that another was making use of, and probably the thing made for another would be found little fitting for his figure of stature and body. But now I have sent you the very wool and the purple from the Lamb, by whom we were redeemed and quickened. When you have received it, you will make it into a coat for yourself according to your own will, and you will rejoice in it as your own private and special garment. And you will exhibit to others also what we have sent, that they themselves may be able to finish it according to their will; so that that old nakedness being covered, they may all bear the garments of Christ robed in the sanctification of heavenly grace.

Cyprian was, by the way, killed for the faith in the persecution ordered by the emperor Valerian. The garment you can make from Scripture is one that you might wear to martyrdom.

The Patient Reader

None of these writers was demanding blind, irrational obedience, as it might seem to us. Nothing so deep and wise as Scripture would reveal all its truths and its true coherence to the casual or uncommitted reader. The patient believer would find that all the apparent problems could be explained.

"The written signs are guiltless; it is the meaning in which they are taken that is to blame," said St. Ambrose of Milan, speaking of the way the Arians interpreted Scripture. (He called them "beings with the outward appearance of men, but inwardly full of brutish folly." In other words, they are not people who are going to understand Scripture correctly.)

For example, the Arians used Jesus' words to the scribes, "Why do you call me good? There is none good but God alone" (Mk 10:18) to prove (so they thought) that Jesus was not fully God. This seemed to be a convincing argument, quoting Jesus himself speaking as if the idea that he were anything like God was ridiculous. I've read modern theologians who also appealed to this verse to say that the early Christians had inflated Jesus' status beyond what Jesus himself claimed.

The Arians had misunderstood Jesus' words, Ambrose asserted. Jesus spoke "with divinely inspired comprehension" of the reason the scribes asked him that question. Notice, said Ambrose, that Jesus didn't say, "There is none good but the Father alone," but "There is none good but God alone." As Jesus was himself God, he was speaking also of himself, but in a way that revealed the scribes' insincerity.

The Lord, then, does not deny His goodness—he rebukes this sort of disciple. For when the scribe said, "Good Master," the Lord answered, "Why do you call me good?" This is to say, "It is not enough to call him good, whom you believe not to be God. Not such do I seek to be my disciples: men who rather consider my manhood and reckon me a good master, than look to my Godhead and believe me to be the good God."

Jesus was saying to them, in effect, "Don't try to butter me up. You think I'm a good man, but that only shows how little you know me, or care to know me."

In the same way, St. Athanasius explained the true meaning of the passages the Arians used to argue that Jesus was a lesser god created by the Father (Acts 2:36; Col 1:15; Heb 1:4; 3:2, for example). They ought to have known from the first verse of St. John's Gospel, he said, that all these verses applied to the point in human history "when at the good pleasure of the Father the Word became man." They do not mean that the Father created a lesser god to do his work, as the Arians claimed, but that he gave his Son a work in human history that these titles ("first born of all creation," for example) describe.

You may or may not agree with Ambrose and Athanasius' readings, but they show how the early Christians read the Scriptures. They knew the real Jesus, and knowing the real Jesus, they knew that he didn't mean what he seems to have meant, and what the Arians insisted he meant. This led them to find other—we would say deeper—explanations of such passages.

Of course, you may say that in the words the early Christians had so carefully gotten right they had the key to Scripture, the key that would reveal the coherence and consistency even of the apparent contradictions; or you may say that they forced the inconvenient pieces of Scripture to fit their preconceived ideas. One can't settle this disagreement with argument, because each side argues as logically as the other.

It is not only a matter of one's first principles, of the things one assumes, but of what one knows. It is a matter of who knows the real Jesus. The early Christians would have insisted that the Bride of Christ knows her Lord.

The First Problem With Yes

I said at the beginning of the chapter that when we try to answer the question, "Isn't Scripture clear enough that we don't need to get the words exactly right?" we find that the answer is "Well, yes and no." I said this because the early Christians' answer seemed to fail in two ways.

The first problem with their belief that "the entire Scriptures, the Prophets, and the Gospels, can be clearly, unambiguously, and harmoniously understood by all," as St. Irenaeus declared, is that even if the Bible's teaching is clear, its readers are fallen men and women whose vision is not very good at all.

Some people just don't understand it. Some of these honestly misunderstand it, while others don't like it but want to keep it and therefore think up ways to change its meaning. Some aren't able to read Scripture at all, and many more who can read aren't able to understand it all or to be sure they understand it rightly.

People are limited, for one thing. Not everyone can read the Scriptures, said St. Cyril of Jerusalem, "some being hindered as to the knowledge of them by want of learning, and others by a want of leisure."

If Scripture is sufficient, St. Vincent asked, why do we need the Church's interpretation? "For this reason: because, owing to the depth of Holy Scripture, all do not accept it in one and the same sense, but one understands its words in one way, another in another; so that it seems to be capable of as many interpretations as there are interpreters."

Second, people are sinful. Those who get the words wrong yet appeal to Scripture rarely say "anything of their own which they do not try to shelter under words of Scripture," Vincent warned. In their writings "you will see an infinite heap of instances, hardly a single page of which does not bristle with plausible quotations from the New Testament or the Old."

Third, the people who are most limited are the easiest prey for those who are sinful. Satan knew that "there is no easier way of effecting his impious purpose than by pretending the authority of Holy Scripture." The more such writers use Scripture, "the more are they to be feared and guarded against," Vincent continued.

For they know that the evil stench of their doctrine will hardly find acceptance with anyone if it be exhaled pure and simple. They sprinkle it over, therefore, with the perfume of heavenly language, in order that one who would be ready to despise human error may hesitate to condemn divine words. They do, in fact, what nurses do when they would prepare some bitter draught for children; they smear the edge of the cup all round with honey, that the unsuspecting child, having first tasted the sweet, may have no fear of the bitter. So too do these act, who disguise poisonous herbs and noxious juices under the names of medicines, so that no one, when he reads the label, suspects the poison.

St. Alexander of Alexandria reported how the Arians would use the verses on one side and ignore those on the other. He opened his explanation of why he had deposed Arius by noting that having "called in question all pious and apostolical doctrine," Arius and his friends had gathered all the passages of Scripture that "speak of his plan of salvation and his humiliation for our sakes, and endeavor[ed] from these to collect the preaching of their impiety, ignoring altogether the passages in which his eternal Godhead and unutterable glory with the Father is set forth."

St. Clement of Alexandria noted that others "will not make use of all the Scriptures, and then they will not quote them entire, nor as the body and texture of prophecy prescribe." They quote selectively and out of context.

[S]electing ambiguous expressions, they wrest them to their own opinions, gathering a few expressions here and there; not looking to the sense, but making use of the mere words. For in almost all the quotations they make, you will find that they attend to the names alone, while they alter the meanings; neither knowing, as they affirm, nor using the quotations they adduce, according to their true nature.

These people, wrote St. Irenaeus, "endeavor to adapt with an air of probability to their own peculiar assertions the parables of the Lord, the sayings of the prophets, and the words of the apostles, in order that their scheme may not seem altogether without support." He compared their use of the Bible to someone taking apart a beautiful picture of the king, made of jewels, and putting the jewels back together to make a bad picture of a dog or a fox (we would say a pig or cockroach), and then claiming this was the beautiful picture of the king.

Wrong Readings

In any case, as soon as someone invents a new way of reading the Bible, other people will believe it, because it will make sense. Remember Gnosticism.

You may, for example, read the four Gospels and think that the Word St. John talks about at the beginning of his Gospel—the Word that was with God and that was God (Jn 1:1)—was that baby in Bethlehem who grew up in Nazareth, gathered a small group of followers, taught for a while, performed miracles, was killed by jealous religious leaders and a cynical government, and then to almost everyone's surprise rose again. It all seems fairly obvious.

But then a Gnostic teacher comes along and tells you that these four Gospels, to the extent you can trust them at all, are really a kind of code or allegory. They don't mean what they seem to mean. You've had a few literature courses and know that stories can mean a lot more than they seem to, and that you only find out the real meaning when you learn which details symbolize what. You remember that poem that bored you to tears until the teacher told you what the flea stood for.

The Gnostic teacher tells you that the Gospels are full of symbols you'll misunderstand or miss completely until you listen to him. This isn't as suspicious a claim as it may appear, put this way.

You've heard enough orthodox teachers find meanings in the text that you hadn't even suspected were there (remember Ambrose). And you've heard orthodox teachers go to some lengths to explain passages like Lot's incest with his daughters by treating them as being symbols or "types" of lessons we need to learn. For that matter, Jesus had to explain some of his par-ables even to his disciples (Mk 4:10-20, for example).

I think, by the way, that the reason we don't feel the attraction of the alternative ways of reading Scriptures as strongly as did the early Christians is not that we know better than they did, but that we don't know Scripture as well as they did. We don't know enough to know that understanding Scripture presents us with some difficult problems.

The Gnostic teacher tells you that the creator is not the God you want to meet, and that Christ was actually a kind of emissary from the real God. He only looked like a human being because looking like a human being was the only way to get people's attention.

Needless to say, not being a real human being, he didn't die on the cross. He left the body he'd borrowed—the one belonging to the good man Jesus—before it died. When Jesus said, "My God, my God, why have you forsaken me?" (Mt 27:46), that was really the borrowed spirit crying out after Christ had left him to return to the real God.

Now that, you think, is something I've always wondered about: how the Son could be abandoned by the Father. And here is a perfectly simple explanation. Suddenly Gnosticism begins to look a lot more believable. You have begun to break the code. Scripture seems to be opening its riches to you in a new way.

Seeing the Code

Now that you begin to see the code, other Gnostic readings begin to make sense too. Some are pretty wild, of course, like the idea that the Gospel of Mark really teaches that Simon of Cyrene was crucified in Jesus' place. But others seem almost common sense, once you understand how the code works and the lessons it is trying to teach.

And some give you insights into Scripture you never would have had otherwise. St. John says that Jesus came off the mountain and went down to Capernaum but did not do any miracles there (Jn 6:14-71). You'd never thought twice about this, but now that your teacher has mentioned it, who could possibly stop God from doing miracles?

John, your teacher tells you, means by saying that Jesus came down from the mountain that the city represented the material world, the lowest world. He could not do anything there because it was a completely material world that could not understand the things of the spirit. This explains why the people seem so dense.

Then the Gnostic teacher might add that the writers of the Gospel stories wrote them to confuse their readers, so that only the truly spiritual reader would see the real meaning. Would a truly spiritual person *really* believe that God would take a human body? your teacher would ask with astonishment. A body that ate and drank and got dirty and, well, had to digest its food? You pass the test for membership if you know this must be wrong. If you like "Silent Night," the Gnostic will not let you in. You feel a little embarrassed that you hadn't seen this before.

In fact, your teacher might continue, who would be so foolish as to believe spiritual truths would be that obvious? (At this point you recall some fairly coarse people in your church. *They* certainly don't deserve to know all this, you think.) And after all, Jesus himself said that narrow is the way that leads to eternal life (Mt 7:14).

If you are vulnerable to ridicule (and most of us are), he may add a few criticisms of the Scriptures themselves. He might suggest that the witnesses were not reliable or that they saw what they wanted to see. The teacher might ask you, as did the Gnostic Celsus, if you believed that all the ancient stories of rising gods were myths yet actually believed that your story of a rising god was true. Put like that, the story of the Resurrection does seem doubtful.

And he might go on to ask, as Celsus did, why you would think a man who couldn't help himself when he was alive could rise again when dead. On top of this, who actually saw him risen? How seriously are we supposed to take the testimony of (in Celsus' words)

a half-frantic woman and some other one, perhaps, of those who were engaged in the same system of delusion, who had either dreamed so, owing to a peculiar state of mind, or under the influence of a wandering imagination had formed to himself an appearance according to his own wishes, which has been the case with numberless individuals; or, which is most probable, one who desired to impress others with this portent, and by such a falsehood to furnish an occasion to impostors like himself.

Everything that Celsus said has been said in heavily footnoted books by learned professors in universities all over the world. They know ten languages and have read everything written between 300 B.C. and A.D. 600. Who are you to argue with them?

Sensible Alternatives

Now this makes sense. That's the problem. Few heretics are ever stupid enough to say something obviously wrong. Christianized Gnostics will take the Bible apart and put it back together again in a way that really does make sense of the evidence, and often give more impressive explanations than most Christian teachers ever think of.

Their systems themselves will build upon certain assumptions most people hold—for example, that God is too great and spiritual to be a baby with a messy bottom—so that the unwary person who comes across their teaching will say, "Aha!" and feel he's found the truth.

These teachings are usually complete in a way the Christian teaching never quite manages to be. The believer, the early

Christians said, sometimes has to believe what he cannot prove. The Christian does not have a compelling answer to questions like "Why does a good God let little children die of leukemia?"

The Christian answer asks you to believe that a good and all-powerful God would allow evil to flourish, and this is hard to do. It is what Christians call a mystery but other people call a fudge, or even a con.

Yet a Gnostic often does offer what seems to be a compelling solution to such problems. That evil flourishes simply isn't God's fault. There is no implausible mystery to be accepted. That a system such as Gnosticism explains so much is a good part of its appeal. It claims to replace faith—and a delusionary faith at that—with knowledge.

The Gnostic's teaching seems to answer all the questions. It drops into place like the last pieces of a puzzle. Anyone who then comes along and says that the puzzle has the wrong design must overcome the pride of the person who has put it together— it was hard to do, after all—and his dislike of taking it apart and starting again.

The Answer to the First Problem

The early Christians gave two answers to this first problem of how fallen people who do not see at all well can know with assurance what Scripture teaches. These were really two aspects of the same answer.

First, as we have seen, they insisted that Christians hold to the Rule of Faith, which put into a few words the faith Scripture conveyed unsystematically in history, poetry, and all the other types of writing it contained. (It is a very long book, remember.)

As we have seen, Scripture could be used to teach a great number of very bad ideas, which Scripture by itself could not refute. The real Jesus was the author of Scripture, and it was from him, through the apostles and those who had passed on their teaching, that we knew what he wanted it to say. When St. Vincent spoke of the "canon of Scripture," he meant not only the official list of books but the Rule (this is what "canon" means) of Faith carried in the Scriptures. He meant not only the code but the codebook.

Because some Christians could not read or understand Scripture, St. Cyril said, "in order that the soul may not perish from ignorance, we comprise the whole doctrine of the faith in a few lines." He insisted that his people memorize this summary, review it often, and hold to it rigidly for the rest of their lives.

Second, the early Christians said to read the whole Bible with a sound mind, devoted to piety and the love of truth, eagerly studying and meditating upon Scripture every day, as St. Irenaeus urged. St. John Chrysostom begged his hearers who "are careful for this life," to

procure books that will be medicines for the soul. If you will not get any other book, get at least the New Testament, the apostolic Epistles, the Acts, the Gospels, for your constant teachers. If grief befall you, dive into them as into a chest of medicines; take thence comfort for your trouble, be it loss, or death, or bereavement of relations. Rather, dive not into them merely, but take them wholly to you; keep them in your mind.

Irenaeus combined the two answers in his instructions to his readers for dealing with the Gnostics who took apart the Scriptures and put it back together in their own way, the ones who turned the king's picture into the picture of a fox or a dog. The Christian "who remains immovable says in his heart the rule of the truth which he received by means of baptism." He'll recognize the Scriptures the Gnostics use, but not "the blasphemous use" to which they put them.

> For, though he will acknowledge the gems, he will certainly not receive the fox instead of the likeness of the king. But when he has restored every one of the expressions quoted to its proper position, and has fitted it to the body of the truth, he will lay bare, and prove to be without any foundation, the figment of these heretics.

What Irenaeus meant, I think, is that the Christian reads the Scripture knowing what it means on all the crucial matters because he has the Rule of Faith. Knowing what it means, he finds that indeed it means what he knew it means. But Scripture does not only confirm the Rule of Faith, it fills in the details. The believer finds that the meaning he sees in Scripture is far more beautiful than he expected. He finds in it the most beautiful picture of his King and Lord.

The Modern Difficulty

Now here is the difficult thing for modern Christians to understand. I have read theologians who claimed that the early

Christians subjected Scripture to the Tradition (in the form of the Rule of Faith), and others (a smaller number) who claimed that they did not think the Tradition was really needed at all because all truths were so easily found in the Scriptures. These are extreme positions, but the writers who asserted them weren't extremists.

They both miss the point. For St. Irenaeus and the other early Christians, the Rule and the Scriptures taught the same truth because they came from the same source: Jesus Christ, speaking through his apostles. They had received both the Rule of Faith and the apostolic writings from the apostles. The truth they had been taught was the same truth they had read.

Christians could trust the Rule of Faith to be apostolic, St. Irenaeus and many others said, because it had been handed down through the unbroken succession of bishops all the way back to the apostles, and therefore to Jesus himself. It was not just received, it was received from men responsible for handing it down unchanged.

It was handed down in a living body guided by the Holy Spirit, who kept that body—the Church—in the truth and pointed it always to the real Jesus. Christians preserve the faith we've received from the Church, which Irenaeus called that "well-grounded system which tends to man's salvation." It always,

by the Spirit of God, renews its youth, as if it were some precious deposit in an excellent vessel, [that] causes the vessel itself containing it to renew its youth also. For this gift of God has been entrusted to the Church, as breath was to the first created man, for this purpose, that all the members receiving it may be vivified; and the [means of] communion with Christ has been distributed throughout it, that is, the Holy Spirit, the earnest of incorruption, the means of confirming our faith, and the ladder of ascent to God.

The early Christians did not divide the word of Scripture from the readings of earlier Christians. "What our fathers said, the same say we," said St. Basil, defending his understanding of the Trinity. ". . . But we do not rest only on the fact that such is the tradition of the Fathers; for they too followed the sense of Scripture."

Many modern Christians can't understand this way of reading Scripture. Instead, many of us tend to separate the authority of Scripture from the authority of Tradition and make one trump the other, in a way the early Christians would never have understood.

The Early Christians' Answer

Let me put this another way. We read the Scriptures assuming that we can just go to the Bible and find out what it says. This presumption is an entirely modern way of thinking that treats even spiritual things as if they were objects of scientific study.

This way of thinking wrongly applies the empirical methods of science to moral and spiritual things. It assumes that you can discern God's Word as easily as you can observe the law of gravity, or more to the point, that *anyone* can discern God's Word as easily as he can observe the law of gravity.

Had anyone put the question to them, the early Christians would have insisted that Scripture could not be understood by anyone who happened to pick up the book. People could so blind themselves that they couldn't see what was in fact right there in front of them.

We saw in the last chapter that St. Irenaeus thought Marcion had so grossly misread Scripture because he hated the God of Scripture, and he hated the God of Scripture because that God told him what to do. We also just saw that St. Ambrose and St. Athanasius thought the Arians had misread Jesus because they didn't know who he is.

All the early Christians would have said the same thing: only the godly will see God. And for them, being godly meant (among other things) submitting yourself to the Rule of Faith. Then you would know the real Jesus and find him in the Scriptures.

But wait, you may be saying, they said (to quote Irenaeus again) that Scripture can "be clearly, unambiguously, and harmoniously understood by all." You may see in the early Christians' appeal to the Rule of Faith and the unwritten Tradition of the Fathers a contradiction. Why would they need to appeal to a rule if Scripture were clear by itself?

Here we have run into one of those places at which they thought very differently from us. It would never have occurred to them that believers would want to read Scripture outside the Rule of Faith they had received at their baptism and shared with all other Christians.

Had St. Irenaeus or St. Cyril or St. Augustine or any of the other early Christians been asked the modern question, I think they would have said something like this: Being a believer who is more formed by the Rule of Faith than you realize, you'll probably get most things right if you read Scripture on your own. But not everything, and some of the things you'll get wrong will probably be very important. You're not all that clever, and you're not all that good.

Then, having warned you that you're likely to get hurt and to hurt others, the early Christians would continue by asking why you would want to do such a thing anyway. They would ask why would you want to read the Scriptures on your own.

If you want to hear the Word of the Lord, you will want to hear it within his Body. If you don't want to hear it within his Body, you probably don't really want to hear it. You are not really a friend of the Lord if you don't care what his other friends think. You want to be inside and outside at the same time.

If by this point you had not fled the room, I think they would finish by trying to explain that the Scriptures and the Rule of Faith, the Bible and the Tradition, couldn't be separated in the way you were trying to do. I'm not sure how they would explain this, because your mind and theirs are so different. But being saints, they would try.

The Second Problem With Yes

I said there were two problems with saying a simple "yes" to the question "Isn't the Bible clear by itself?" The second problem is that the Bible doesn't always put its teachings in the form that later Christians found they needed. This is a very difficult question, because it raises all those questions of development that divide Christians, such as the papacy and the sacraments and the place of Mary. I intend to step quietly around the questions, but I will give a safe example from the fourth century.

The early Christians believed that Jesus was completely God in every sense that mattered and completely man in every sense that mattered. They received this in the Rule of Faith and they read this in the Scriptures. They gave their lives to Jesus—and sometimes died under torture for him—because they believed him to be the Son of God who was born of the Virgin Mary and was made man. Everyone (believers, I mean) knew this, and the Church went about its work.

But soon enough someone came along and said, "Yes, that's all true. I believe that with all my heart. But his being completely God in every sense that matters doesn't mean that he was quite the same thing as God, because that would make God himself *less* God. This we certainly don't want to do. I've got a safer way of describing how the Father and the Son relate to each other, and I've found it in the apostolic writings." The man who said this was an influential priest and an eloquent preacher.

At this point (we are obviously talking about Arius) the orthodox or Catholic party got upset. They knew he was wrong, they argued against him with real brilliance, they carefully showed from the apostolic writings that Jesus is equal to God the Father. They could all read the opening of John's Gospel, for heaven's sake.

Ah, said Arius and his friends, of course you can read Scripture that way. But how do you explain all the times that Jesus stressed his inferiority to the Father? Your system doesn't account for those passages.

The Catholics did not doubt they were right, so the bishop went ahead and excommunicated Arius when he refused to recant. Yet the apostolic writings themselves didn't give them any exact, convenient, unmistakable way of making the distinction between the Christian view and Arius' innovation. They knew they had to get the words right on this matter, but Scripture did not give them the right word. It did not give them a knock-out punch.

The Answer to the Second Problem

The bishops gathered at the Council of Nicaea in 325 settled on the word *homoousion*, meaning "of one essence" or "of the same essence." They adapted the word from the philosophy of the day. It was not a biblical word, and many of the Arians objected to it (they said) on that ground. In fact, many of the Catholics did not want to accept it for the same reason.

But in the end, "of one essence" was the only word that would do. The teaching of Scripture was clear, taken as a whole and read with the mind of the Church, but a word taken from outside Scripture was needed to say neatly what Scripture taught in its hundreds of thousands of words. As St. Athanasius wrote when the Arians, having lost at Nicaea, claimed that they needed more councils "for the faith's sake":

> Divine Scripture is sufficient above all things; but if a council be needed on the point, there are the proceedings of the Fathers, for the Nicene bishops did not neglect this matter, but stated the doctrine so exactly, that persons reading their words honestly, cannot but be reminded by them of the religion of Christ announced in divine Scripture.

The word the bishops took from Greek philosophy was the word they needed. They would all have said that the canon of Scripture is complete, and sufficient of itself for everything, and more than sufficient, and that among the things plainly laid down in Scripture are to be found all matters that concern faith and the manner of life.

They would said have this, and then added that some people needed help in understanding Scripture, and other people needed correction. On the question of Jesus' relation to his Father, this help and correction they found in the word meaning "of the same essence." They would have liked to have avoided the whole fight, and not even used a word they couldn't take from Scripture, but when they needed a knock-out punch, they found one.

The Real Jesus

"Isn't Scripture clear enough that we don't need to get the words exactly right?" is one of those great questions to which the answer is "Well, yes and no, but more no than yes." In the life of the Christian, the Word and the right words cannot be separated. Without one, you do not have the other.

The real Jesus shines brightly from the Scriptures, from the Old Testament to the New. But to see him there, the early Christians believed, you have to read them with the right heart—not just with the right attitude or paradigm or mental tools, but with a whole way of living, including the moral life the Church requires.

If you lived this way, you would naturally accept the Rule of

Faith and the words the early Christians found to explain what is there. All those who truly wanted to hear God's Word would submit themselves to those of his servants who had been entrusted with the truth and had carefully passed it on.

The Christian who lives the Christian life will see clearly and will not be fooled by those who speak the wrong words. "None of the devices of the devil shall be hidden from you," said St. Ignatius of Antioch,

> if, like Paul, you perfectly possess that faith and love towards Christ which are the beginning and the end of life. The beginning of life is faith, and the end is love. And these two being inseparably connected together, perfect the man of God, while all other things which are requisite to a holy life follow after them.

All this St. Athanasius emphasized at the very end of his work *On the Incarnation*. When he finished explaining to his friend Macarius why the Son of God had become man, he insisted that Macarius test his arguments by studying the Scriptures. But to find the answer in Scripture Macarius had to be a certain sort of man, a certain sort of Christian.

> For the searching and right understanding of the Scriptures there is need of a good life and a pure soul, and for Christian virtue to guide the mind to grasp, so far as human nature can, the truth concerning God the Word.... Anyone who wants to look at sunlight naturally wipes his eye clear first, in order to make, at any rate, some approximation to the purity of that on which he looks; and a per-

son wishing to see a city or country goes to the place in order to do so. Similarly, anyone who wishes to understand the mind of the sacred writers must first cleanse his own life, and approach the saints by copying their deeds.

By the saints, Athanasius meant the apostolic writers and those who have passed on to us the apostolic teaching. As he had said earlier in the book, he was able to teach only because he had "learned from inspired teachers who read the Scriptures and became martyrs for the Godhead of Christ." In the love and life of the saints is not only understanding but salvation.

Thus united to them [the saints] in the fellowship of life, he will both understand the things revealed to them by God and, thenceforth escaping the peril that threatens sinners in the judgment, will receive that which is laid up for the saints in the kingdom of heaven.

SIX

THE LAST WORD

In his wonderful book *Letters to a Niece*, Frederic von Hügel reminded her of the eighteenth-century historian Edward Gibbon's "far too influential gibe at the Arian controversy—that it was all a silly squabble concerning a diphthong." The words for "same essence" and "like essence" differed by only one letter, and Gibbon sneered at the Christians for fighting over so meaningless a difference.

Gibbon was the silly one. He

thus confounded rich, far-reaching, live differences with their ultimate reduction to technical terms. You might as well declare [of] a controversy turning upon one million pounds sterling that [the] presence or absence [of the money] was but a wrangle over the numerical sign—the vertical stroke—of 1. Since, on the one side, men wrangled "000,000" and, on the other, men wrangled "1,000,000."

Gibbon's famous remark is tiresome and silly, and unworthy of someone who was as astonishingly intelligent and learned as he was. He knew better, I am sure, and I do wonder how much he simply refused to see the reality to which the right word pointed. It is easier to make jokes about words than risk meeting the real Jesus.

People running away from Jesus often look like the criminals running away from the police in movies: running into walls, knocking down trash cans, tripping over sticks and cats, ripping their clothes, falling in garbage, gasping for breath. The one fleeing has lost his dignity and sometimes his reason.

It is easier to make jokes, but it is not wise. The man Gibbon was unwilling to meet will someday come again in glory to judge the living and the dead (the latter now including Gibbon). There is always a point at which the one fleeing Jesus comes to a dead-end alley and finds that he cannot escape him. He has to turn and face him, but because he has run away, he now meets Jesus not as a friend, but as a judge.

I hope you have seen in the witness of the early Christian saints the reasons for getting the words you say about him exactly right. In the words we say about him we are drawing his picture, and we want the picture to be as complete and accurate as we can make it. If a diphthong gives us another detail, we will include the diphthong.

We do this, as the early Christians did, not just to make sure we recognize our Lord and Savior, and are not fooled by all the imitations and frauds. We do this because we love him, and want to look upon his face.

SOURCES

I have put the sources in this form to help those irritated or even intimidated (and a surprising number of people are) by the sight of lots of little numbers dotted up and down the pages. They are arranged by section heading in the order they appear, to make it easier for readers to find a quote from the middle of a chapter. Additional comments are indented.

Unless noted, all the quotations from the early Christians are taken from the thirty-eight-volume Edinburgh Edition of the writings of the early Church fathers, which includes three series:

Alexander Roberts and James Donaldson, eds., *The Ante-Nicene Fathers: Translations of the Writings of the Fathers Down to A.D. 325.* Grand Rapids, Michigan: Eerdmans, 1987 (reprint), 10 vols.

Philip Schaff, ed., *A Select Library of the Nicene and Post-Nicene Fathers of the Christian Church* (First Series). Grand Rapids, Michigan: Eerdmans, 1988 (reprint), 14 vols.

Philip Schaff, ed., *A Select Library of the Nicene and Post-Nicene Fathers of the Christian Church* (Second Series). Grand Rapids, Michigan: Eerdmans, 1986 (reprint), 14 vols.

I have sometimes updated the language or turned rhetorical questions into statements.

This set of volumes is still available in print from Eerdmans Publishing Company. It is also available on CD-ROM from Logos Research Systems (http://logos.com) and Harmony Media (www.harmonymediainc.com). The Christian Classics Ethereal Library (CCEL) offers all volumes online (http://www.ccel.org/fathers2/info.html) except the index volume for the Ante-Nicene series.

Chapter One
The Saints' Words

Writing After Persecution: For a summary of Irenaeus' teaching, see *The Scandal of the Incarnation*, selected by Hans Urs von Balthasar (San Francisco: Ignatius, 1990).

Sanctus' Death: The story is given in a letter from the survivors, recorded in Eusebius, *Church History* 4.1.

For more on the persecution of the early Christians, see W.H.C. Frend, *Martyrdom and Persecution in the Early Church* (Grand Rapids, Michigan: Baker, 1981).

The Early Saints: Irenaeus, *Against Heresies* 3.3.4 [on Polycarp].

The Scholars and the Saints: See, for example, the scholars quoted in the "Frontline" series "From Jesus to Christ." The webpage "Diversity of Early Christianity" (http://www.pbs.org/wgbh/pages/frontline/shows/religion/first/diversity.html) includes several arguments to this effect. Professor Elaine Pagels of Princeton University said, for example, that in the second century "there was no list of agreed gospels. There was no list of agreed doctrines. And there was no agreed-upon structure" (http://www.pbs.org/wgbh/pages/frontline/shows/religion/story/heretics.html). She can make this claim by including everyone of the day who claimed to be a Christian, which is to say, she assumes that there was not an authentic Gospel passed on from the Lord and his apostles that distinguished Christians from those who wanted only to claim the name.

The Real Problem: Frederic von Hügel, *Letters to a Niece* (London: J.M. Dent & Sons, 1928) [on "pinning down" the Faith]; G.K. Chesterton, *Heretics* (New York: Dodd, Mead, & Company, 1905), 285-86 [chapter 20].

Submission to the Saints: C.S. Lewis, *Letters to Malcolm* (New York: Harcourt, Brace, Jovanovich, 1964), 13.

Chapter Two
Words to Die For

G. K. Chesterton, "The Crime of the Communist" in *The Father Brown Omnibus* (New York: Dodd, Mead, and Company, 1951), 611.

The Modern Mind: Ignatius, *Epistle to the Smyrnaeans* 1 [on Jesus]; Athanasius, *Against the Arians* 3.4, 3.11; Athanasius, *Discourse Against the Arians* 2.14 [Arian uses of Scripture].

For Arius' theology see his letters to Bishops Eusebius and Alexander of Alexandria and his song *Thalia*, in J. Stevenson, ed., *A New Eusebius* (London: S.P.C.K., 1987 [new edition revised by W.H.C. Frend]), 322-32.

They Fight On: Jerome, *Dialogue Against the Luciferians*, 19.

Gnosticism's Challenge: Elaine Pagels, "Gnostics and Other Heretics," from the "Frontline" series "From Jesus to Christ" (http://www.pbs.org/wgbh/pages/frontline/shows/religion/story/heretics.html).

See also Irenaeus, *Against Heresies* 1.6.3, 1.25.2, 3.11.1, and 1.26.1.

Gnostic morals: Saturnilus, quoted in Hippolytus, *Refutation of All Heresies* 7.21 [on marriage].

The Gnostic Mistake: Irenaeus, *Against Heresies* 1.26.1 [on Cerinthus].

The Case of Marcion: Irenaeus, *Against Heresies* 1.27.3 and 1.28.1.

I took much of the description of Marcionism from Stuart G. Hall, *Doctrine and Practice in the Early Church* (Grand Rapids, Michigan: Eerdmans, 1991), 37-39, 97. For another description, see Patrick Reardon, "Marcionism Then and Now," *Touchstone*, March 2000 <www.touchstonemag.com/docs/issues/13.2docs/13.2pg18.html >.

Marcion's Heaven: Irenaeus, *Against Heresies* 5 and 1.27.2.

A Modern Example: John Macquarrie, *Principles of Christian Theology* (New York: Scribners, 1977), 31, 278, 282, 286, 294, 288.

Macquarrie's salvation: C.S. Lewis, "Myth Became Fact," *God in the Dock* (Grand Rapids, Michigan: Eerdmans, 1970), 63-67; John Henry Newman, "The Tamworth Reading Room" [sixth letter], *Essays and Sketches*, vol. 2 (New York: Longmans, Green, and Co., 1948), 204.

No Lone Rangers: Leo, *Letter to Flavian, Commonly Called "The Tome,"* Letter 28.1.

The Dean Again: G.K. Chesterton, "The Crime of the Communist" in *The Father Brown Omnibus* (New York: Dodd, Mead, and Company, 1951), 611.

Chapter Three
Loving the Right Words

Ignatius, *Epistle to the Ephesians* 20.

Rule of Faith: Athanasius, *Letter to Serapion* 1.28, quoted in Kelly, *Early Christian Doctrines* (San Francisco: Harper & Row, 1978 [revised edition]), 31; Ignatius, *Epistle to the Ephesians* 17; Polycarp, *Epistle to the Philippians* 7; Irenaeus, *Against Heresies* 3.15.1 (he also uses the phrase in 3.11.1 and 4.35.4); ibid., 1.10.2; Irenaeus, *Epidexis* 6, quoted in Kelly, *Early Christian Creeds,* third edition (London: Longman, 1972), 77; Tertullian, *Prescription Against Heretics* 7; Irenaeus, *Against Heresies* 1.10.1; Tertullian, *Prescription Against Heretics* 13; Origen, *On First Principles* preface 4-10; Gregory of Nyssa, *Against Eunomius* 4.6.

Many other Fathers offered their versions of the Rule of Faith: for example, Ignatius, *Letter to the Trallians* 9 and *Letter to the Smyrnaeans* 1.3; *Martyrdom of the Holy Martyrs* 1, quoting Justin Martyr on trial for his life. They also wrote about it in other ways, as when Irenaeus wrote that "the tradition from the apostles does thus exist in the Church, and is permanent among us" (*Against Heresies* 3.5.1).

Drawing From the Bank: *Epistle to Diognetus* 12, quoted in Michael Green, *Evangelism and the Early Church* (Grand Rapids, Michigan: Eerdmans, 1960), 135; Irenaeus, *Fragments* 2; Irenaeus, *Against Heresies* Book 3.4.1; ibid., I.10.2; ibid., 3.4.1; ibid., 3.4.2; Cyril of Jerusalem, *Catechetical Lectures* 4.12.

Beyond the Pale: Irenaeus, *Against Heresies* 4.33.7; ibid., 3.1.2; ibid., 4.26.2 (see also 1.22.1); Clement, *Stromateis* 7.16; Basil, *On the Holy Spirit* 10.

Loving the Story: J.N.D. Kelly, *Early Christian Creeds,* 81 and 75.

Evangelism: *Epistle to Diognetus,* in B.J. Kidd, ed., *Documents Illustrative of the History of the Church,* vol. I (London: SPCK, 1920), 7.

Baptism: Hippolytus, *Apostolic Tradition,* ed. Gregory Dix and Henry Chadwick (London: Alban, 1992), 21.12-18.

No Wiggle Room: Hippolytus, *Apostolic Tradition* 19.2.

Delivered From Idols: Basil, *On the Holy Spirit* 10.

Doctrinal Prayers: *The Epistle Concerning the Martyrdom of Polycarp* 14. Some scholars think this prayer was invented by later Christians, but even if it was it still shows what they thought about such things.

Flying the Flag: Eusebius, *Church History,* introduction to book 5; *Epistle to Diognetus* 7.

Nailed to the Cross: Ignatius, *Letter to the* Smyrnaeans 1.

Doctrinal Encouragements: Ignatius, *Epistle to Polycarp* 3.

Doctrinal Instructions: Polycarp, *Letter to the Philippians* 6-7. The Scriptures he quotes are, in order, 1 Peter 4:3; Matthew 6:13; and Matthew 26:41.

Patrick's Confession: St. Patrick, *The Confession of St. Patrick.* Translated from the Latin by Ludwig Bieler << http://www.ccel.org/p/patrick/confession/confession.html >>.

Chapter Four
Hating the Wrong Words

The Apostolic Style: Irenaeus, *Against Heresies* 3.3.4.

Enemies of Faith: Irenaeus, *Against Heresies* 3.3.4; Irenaeus, *Fragments* 2 (the story is also told in Irenaeus' *Letter to Florinus,* in Eusebius, *Church History* 5.20.6-8); Irenaeus, *Against Heresies* 3.3.4; ibid., 1,28.1 [on heretics as gurus]; ibid., 3.3.4.

The Fathers often ascribed heresy to sin. Clement, for example, wrote of those who, "giving themselves up to pleasures, wrest Scripture, in accordance with their lusts" (*Stromateis* 7.16). The lust may be a consuming desire for fame or approval or power as much as for sexual experiences.

Marcion's Errors: Justin Martyr, *First Apology* 26 and 58; Vincent of Lerins, *Commonitory* 68 (his definition of the Catholic Church is found in section 6); Irenaeus, *Against Heresies* 1.27.3; ibid. 1.preface.2; ibid. 5.26.2.

Abusive Tertullian: Tertullian, *Against Marcion,* Book I.1.

Samosatan Resistance: Theodoret, *Ecclesiastical History* 4.13.

For other stories of lay resistance, see the stories of the laity of Amasia in Sozomen, *Ecclesiastical History* 7.2., and of the ambitious Fronto in Benedict, *Life of St. Basil,* quoted in John Henry Newman, *The Arians of the Fourth Century* (London: Longmans, Green, and Co., 1897), 458-59. For renouncing the faith in order to be made bishop by the Arians, Fronto became known as "the execration of all Armenia."

The five famous Eusebiuses, as listed in the *Oxford Dictionary of the*

Christian Church (2nd ed., rev.) were: Eusebius of Caesarea (the one often called the father of Church history), Eusebius the bishop of Emesa (a Semi-Arian), Eusebius the bishop of Nicomedia (an Arian leader), St. Eusebius the bishop of Vercelli (exiled for the faith and suggested as the author of the Athanasian Creed), and St. Eusebius the bishop of Samosata (also exiled for the faith and a friend of St. Basil the Great).

Other Examples: Basil, *Letters* 92.2; ibid. 242.2; Hilary, *Letter to Constantius* I.1.2, quoted in Newman's *The Arians of the Fourth Century*, 463-64.

Hilary's defense: Hilary, *On the Councils* 3, 10, and 2; the text of the "Blasphemy of Sirmium" is given in Kelly, *Early Christian Creeds*, 286-87.

It is useful to note that St. Athanasius did not reject the "Semi-Arians," the moderates who rejected Arianism but were for a time politically entangled with the Arians, and some of whose bishops signed the "Blasphemy." They thought the Nicaean position confused the Father and the Son, and that Athanasius and the rest had responded to the Arian mistake by going too far in the other direction. They preferred the word "of like essence" (*homoiousios*) to the Nicaean "of one essence" (*homoousios*). As Athanasius himself wrote, those who doubted the word "of the same essence" but accepted everything said at Nicaea were not enemies, "Ario-maniacs," or "opponents of the Fathers." With them, "we discuss the matter as brothers with brothers, who mean what we mean, and dispute only about the word" (*The Councils of Ariminum and Selucia* 3.41).

"Knowing Not God": Hilary, *On the Trinity* 8.6.

No Honest Mistakes: Ambrose, *On the Faith* 2.89; Ignatius, *Letter to the Smyrnaeans* 4.

A Caution: Basil, *Letters* 92.2.

In the Midst of Wolves: John Chrysostom, *Homilies on Matthew*, Homily 33.1.3.

Triumphant Sheep: John Chrysostom, *Homilies on Matthew*, Homily 33.1.3; Gregory of Nazianzus, *Oration* 6.20, quoted in Jean Danielou, "The Fathers and Christian Unity," *Eastern Churches Quarterly* XVI.1 (1964): 14-15.

The Fathers teach us that two things must be done in ecumenical talks, Fr. Danielou wrote: "interpret the other's opinion in the most favorable light" and "make no concession whatsoever on matters of truth," for "if it is possible to sin through pride and intransigence, then it is also possible to sin by being careless and conceding on matters of principle."

His Wounds: Sulpicius Severus, *The Life of St. Martin* 24.

Chapter Five
The Word and the Words

The Saints' Yes: Irenaeus, *Against Heresies* 2.27.3; Vincent of Lerins, *Commonitory* 5; Cyril, *Catechetical Lectures* 4.17; Athanasius, *Against the Heathen* 1.1.3; Athanasius, *Defense of the Nicene Definition* 32; Basil, *Epistle* 189.3; Augustine, *On Christian Doctrine* 2.14; John Chrysostom, *Homilies on 2 Thessalonians,* Third Homily [on 2 Thess. 2:5]; John Chrysostom, *Homilies on Colossians,* Ninth Homily [on Col. 3:16-17]; John Chrysostom, *Homilies on 2 Thessalonians* 3 [on 2 Thess. 2:5].

The Source: Ignatius, *Letter to the Smyrnaeans* 5.1 and 7.2; *2 Clement* 2.4; Justin Martyr, *Dialogue with Trypho* 49.5; *Barnabas* 4.14; Clement, *Stromateis* 7.16; Irenaeus, *Against Heresies* 3.1.1; Athanasius, *Defense of the Nicene Definition* 4. (The first four references are taken from Kelly, *Early Christian Doctrines,* 56.)

The Reader: Irenaeus, *Against Heresies* 2.27.2; Clement, *Stromateis* 7.16; Basil, quoted in Newman, *Arians,* 160; John Chrysostom, quoted in Newman, *Arians,* 160; Justin Martyr, *First Apology* 19 (he is quoting Matthew 19:26 and 10:28); Cyprian, *Treatise XI: Exhortation to Martyrdom* 3.

The Patient Reader: Ambrose of Milan, *Exposition of the Christian Faith* 2.1; Athanasius, *Discourse Against the Arians* 2.14.

In the same way, Hilary noted that "the heretics [he was talking about the Arians] when beset by authoritative passages in Scripture are wont only to grant that the Son is like the Father in might while they deprive him of similarity of nature" (*On the Councils* 19). In other words, they granted the obvious so that they could claim to be following the Scriptures and yet still deny the Nicaean understanding of the Son. "By confused and involved expressions the heretics very frequently elude the truth and secure the ears of the unwary by the mere sound of common words, such as the titles Father and Son," he noted a few paragraphs later (20).

The First Problem With Yes: Cyril, *Catechetical Lectures* 5.12; Vincent, *Commonitory* 5, 64, 67, 65; Alexander, *First Epistle on the Arian Heresy* 1; Clement, *Stromateis* 7.16; Irenaeus, *Against Heresies* 1.8.1.

Wrong Readings: Irenaeus, *Against Heresies* 4.31 [lesson of Lot]; Irenaeus, *Against Heresies* 1.24.4, quoted in Robert Grant, *The Earliest Lives of Jesus* (San Francisco: Harper & Brothers, 1961), 10 (the gnostic Basilides interpreted Mark 15:21-5 as describing Simon's crucifixion); Origen, *Commentary on John* 10.48-59, quoted in Kelly, *Early Christian Doctrines,* 70 (the Gnostic Heracleon interpreted "down from the mountain" as meaning his entering the material world).

Seeing the Code: Celsus, as quoted by Origen in *Contra Celsum* 2.55.

The Answer to the First Problem: Cyril, *Catechetical Lectures* 5.12; John Chrysostom, *Homilies on 2 Thessalonians* 3; Irenaeus, *Against Heresies* 1.9.4.

The Modern Difficulty: Irenaeus, *Against Heresies* 3.24.1; Basil, *On the Holy Spirit* 7.

The Answer to the Second Problem: Athanasius, *The Councils of Ariminum and Seleucia* 1.6. The Fathers knew the dangers of using such a word; see Hilary, *On the Councils* 67-70.

The Real Jesus: Ignatius, *Epistle to the Ephesians* 14; Athanasius, *On the Incarnation,* 56-57, translation by "A Religious of C.S.M.V." (London: Mowbray, 1953), 95-96.

Chapter Six
The Last Word

Frederic von Hügel, *Letters to a Niece* (London: J. M. Dent & Sons, 1928), 51.